KATMAI

National Park and Preserve
Alaska

Jean Bodeau

Alaska Natural History Association and
Greatland Graphics
Anchorage, Alaska

JOHN TUCKEY

Author
Jean Bodeau is an inveterate adventurer who enjoys sea kayaking, hiking and back country skiing. She has traveled throughout India, Nepal and Latin America and makes her living as a groundwater hydrologist.

The Alaska Natural History Association is a non-profit organization dedicated to enhancing the public's understanding and conservation of Alaska's natural, cultural and historical resources by working in cooperation with land management agencies and other educational organizations throughout Alaska.

Available by mail for $14.95 each plus $3.00 per order shipping from: Alaska Public Lands Information Center, 605 West Fourth Avenue, Anchorage, Alaska 99501.

Printing
Lorraine Press

Editing
MeiMei Evans

Design and production
Edward Bovy

Cartography
Carol Belenski

Chapter illustrations
Kim Mincer

Wildlife illustrations
Susan Steinacher

Photos
Copyrighted by the photographers or contributing organizatons as credited.

Front cover
Brown bear and cubs, Brooks Falls (Gary Lackie)

Back cover
Mt. Mageik (Edward Bovy)

Library of Congress catalogue card number: 92-071232

KATMAI

National Park and Preserve, Alaska

C O N T E N T S

Part 2: INSIDE KATMAI

Maps

Acknowledgements

I am grateful to everyone who helped with the production of this book. I offer heartfelt thanks to Ed Bovy of Greatland Graphics for his enthusiasm and persistence in publishing this book and editing the manuscript, and to Frankie Barker of the Alaska Natural History Association for supporting the project from the start.

Katmai Superintendent Alan Eliason, Mark Wagner, Steve Hurd, Ron Squibb, Tammy Olson, Jeanne Schaaf, Roger Harritt and Bonnie Houston, all with the National Park Service, reviewed the manuscript. MeiMei Evans edited the manuscript.

Tina Neal and Game McGimsey of the U.S. Geological Survey, Ron Hood of Becharof National Wildlife Refuge, Larry Aumiller of McNeil River State Game Sanctuary, Sonny Petersen and Perry Mollan of Katmailand, and photographer Fred Hirschmann also reviewed the text or provided information.

The hospitality of the volunteer campground hosts, Bill and Pat Allan, and the kindness of park and concessionaire staff members Lisa Davis, Linda Marr, Jennifer Gape, David Nemeth, Rick Potts, and Bo Bennett made my stay in Katmai more enjoyable.

Thanks to Antonia Fowler and Lisa Johnson, who joined me on backcountry trips in Katmai. And lastly, thanks to John Tuckey and Lenny for encouraging me and putting up with me throughout the writing of this book.

Jean Bodeau

Long ago, in a place far away
The sky was as blue as the sea
And the sea was as blue as the sky
And the earth was green
And in love with them both.

Anonymous
Baked Mountain Cabin Journal

Baked Mountain Camp and Mt. Martin.
NATIONAL GEOGRAPHIC SOCIETY

CHAPTER 1

Introduction

Katmai. The meaning of the word is lost, except for the mountain, the river, and the abandoned village that wear the name. Perhaps it meant long curved claws gleaming in the sunshine, shaggy coat stretched over muscled shoulders, penetrating brown eyes ... a thumping heart. This land is home to the brown bear, whose trails dissect the woods, the wetlands, the snowy peaks. Brown bear threads through this country as we do our homes: familiar, possessive, year after year. We, like Goldilocks, are the guests.

Katmai could mean a touching of extremes. It is a lasagna of overlapping con-trasting worlds, layered in time and character. The fiery volcanos of the Aleutian Range erupt through the crevassed blue of glacier ice. The Alaska Peninsula, southwestern stub of the vast interior of Alaska, and the rugged giants of the Alaska Range give way to the Aleutian island chain. Descending to the north, the volcanos flatten into the largest system of lakes and rivers in the national park system before reaching the salmon-rich waters of Bristol Bay. To the south, they plunge to the rugged coastline of the cold and stormy Shelikof Straits.

Often a meeting place of cultures, Katmai was home to Eskimo, Indian, and Aleut in the days before white people arrived. *Barabara* depressions pockmark the ground at Brooks Camp, remnants of the

Hikers in Valley of Ten Thousand Smokes ponder fresh bear tracks. EDWARD BOVY

houses where Natives of millennia past crafted slate tools by the light of seal-oil lamps. Virtually every cabin at Brooks Camp sits atop buildings or relics of these ancient people.

Hikers follow trails tramped into existence by trappers who traded with the Russians during the days of Bering and Shelikov, or by the first whites who came to Katmai looking for wealth in rocks and pelts. All traces of Katmai village were buried in the ashfall of 1912, the eruption that drew the attention of the world to Katmai. In this largest blast of the twentieth century, ash spewed from the earth, plunging the region into a viscous blackness for three days as volcanic debris rained down over thousands of square miles.

Through all these worlds weaves a chain of brown bear footprints, linking alpine tundra and sockeye salmon, Eskimo hunter and fisherman, in an intricate web. Brown bears greeted the first humans, fishing in the rivers then as they do today. They plod across Katmai Pass from the windswept coast to the Naknek lowlands, tracking dust from the Valley of Ten Thousand Smokes into Brooks Camp. Their tracks cross ours, entwining our footprints through time in the lavish dimensions of this land. Our timid hearts and twentieth century lives become irreversibly woven into this earthy tapestry of Katmai, whether or not we feel it. Whether or not we accept it. Perhaps Katmai means this: a chance to sense the threads that tie our world to the brown bears', binding us together before we arrive in Katmai, and even after we leave.

The Ukak River is carving a spectacular canyon in the ash near Three Forks. KIM HEACOX

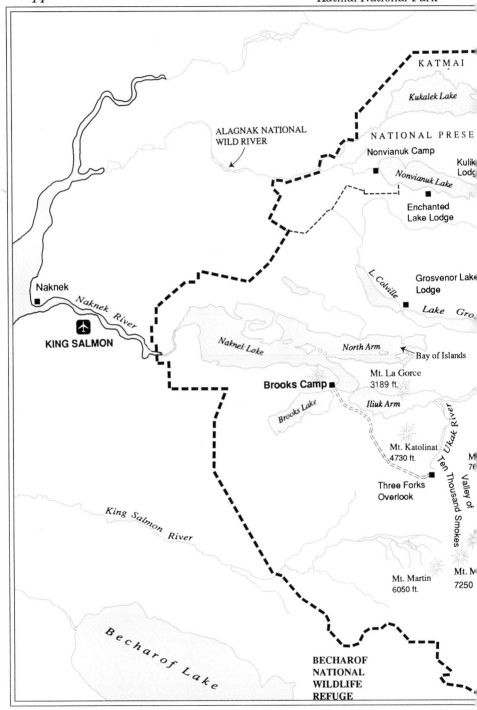

Map 1. Katmai National Park

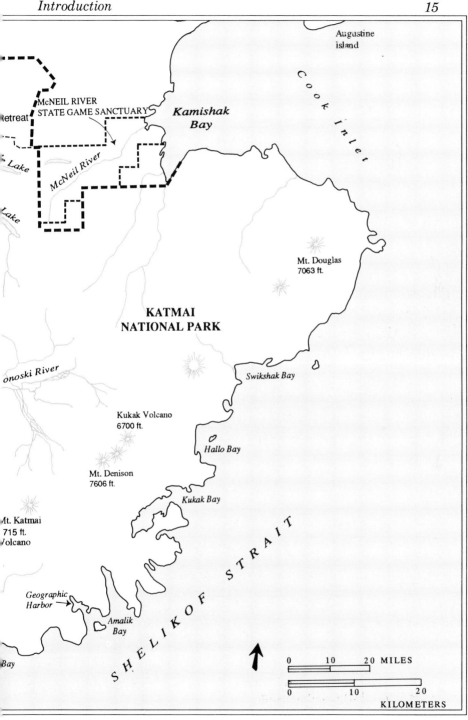

Augustine island

C o o k   I n l e t

McNEIL RIVER
STATE GAME SANCTUARY

Retreat

*Kamishak
Bay*

Lake

McNeil River

Lake

Mt. Douglas
7063 ft.

**KATMAI
NATIONAL PARK**

onoski River

Swikshak Bay

Kukak Volcano
6700 ft.

Hallo Bay

Mt. Denison
7606 ft.

Kukak Bay

Mt. Katmai
715 ft.
Volcano

S H E L I K O F   S T R A I T

Geographic
Harbor

*Amalik
Bay*

Bay

0   10   20 MILES

0   10   20

KILOMETERS

Brown bears know exactly where the fish are jumping at Brooks Falls.
GARY LACKIE

CHAPTER 2

A Tale of Red Salmon
and Brown Bear

What is man without the beasts? If all the beasts were gone, man would die from great loneliness of spirit, for whatever happens to the beast also happens to the man. All things are connected. Whatever befalls the earth befalls the sons of the earth.

Chief Seathl, Duwamish Tribe
State of Washington, 1855

Into the Gaping Maw

Slim odds, I thought, when I first watched a sow grizzly poised on the rim of Brooks Falls, that a fish will actually leap into her mouth. Oh, I'd seen the photos — bears with sockeye plugged into their mouths like lightbulbs — but surely, I reasoned, they use those enormous claw-tipped paws to help with the catch. Not so. During my first half hour at Brooks Falls, I watched this one bear stand-ing in the same spot catch four fish in a row this way. Had she moved her feet, the swift cur-rent could have knocked her into the whirlpool below the lip of the falls. So she stood there, feet planted and jaws agape, waiting for the salmon that would be her next meal.

As everyone who visits Brooks Falls quickly discov-ers, there are as many fishing styles as there are bears. Some bears wade shoulder-deep in the river, eyeballs submerged and searching for fish, pouncing like a cat when they spot one. Others forage downstream for injured fish or leftover pieces that drift down from the falls. One large male even learned to dive, an unusual and efficient technique that enabled him to catch fish where other bears couldn't.

What goes on at Brooks Falls and other rivers throughout the Katmai region each summer is the age-old weaving of these two species lives.

Only a few months earlier, thousands of miles separated salmon from bear. The salmon swam in the cold, nutrient-rich currents of the Pacific Ocean along with millions of other fish from around the Pacific Rim —Japan, Siberia, California, Alaska.

For two to three years most lived in the ocean, feeding at first on microscopic organisms, but growing to depend on crustaceans, fish, and squid.

When the salmon received the biological signal to depart the cold waters of the Pacific and swim toward Bristol Bay, Alaska, the brown bears of Katmai were just emerging from their dens. Burrows in mountain flanks, each den harbored one hibernating bear or a sow with cubs.

After emerging from their dens in early May, the bears ate very little for the first few weeks. They nibbled shoots of sedge, horsetail, and other spring plants. Some hunted moose or caribou calves, or animals left weak by the winter. They followed squirrel scent, clawing away the moist earth to locate the rodents, and foraged on the previous year's berries.

They dropped down from the mountains and, after the salmon finished their marathon swim to freshwater, the bears found sockeye salmon swarming up the river, predictably, as they had for centuries. Bear and salmon met once again.

Fattened on calorie-rich salmon, the bears of Katmai and the Alaska Peninsula are among the largest in the world. Slightly larger than the females, males weigh 400 to 1,000 pounds, although exceptionally large individuals may reach 1,400 pounds and stand up to eleven feet in height.

The shaggy fur of brown bears can be any shade from luminous blonde to chocolate brown or almost black. Tipped with silver, the coat may appear "grizzled," or grayish. In the past, biologists characterized brown and grizzly bears as different subspecies, since brown bears, which live near the coast, grow so much larger than grizzly bears, which live in the interior. Both bears are now recognized as *Ursus arctos horribilis*, with the difference in size attributed to the abundance of salmon near the coast.

An estimated two thousand of these massive brown bears live in Katmai National Park; the park itself is only a portion of the prime bear habitat on the Alaska Peninsula.

Bear Rapport

At Brooks Falls, a large dark male bear with a scarred right hip loped out of the spruce forest. He sloshed through the rushing clear water toward the lip of the falls, eyes fixed on the young subadult with a two-tone head staring into the water. This was the large boar's favorite fishing hole, and he didn't care to share it with the younger bear.

One glimpse of the large boar coming his way was enough to send the young bear scrambling for shore. He joined two other juveniles his size pacing the grassy river bank.

At the same time, a large blonde sow herded three tiny cubs downstream. Fiercely protective, she put a large expanse of water between her cubs and the boar, finally stopping at a beach. The cubs splashed in the water, tiny heads bobbing in the sunshine, while their mother swatted salmon in the shallows.

While brown bears do not form packs or herds, as do other more social animals, they do interact socially in a variety of ways. Cubs stay with their mothers for two to three years after birth.

After they leave their mothers, adolescent bear siblings may stay with each other for a few additional years. Subadults, those bears from about 2-1/2 to 3-1/2 years old, are likely to hunt, fish, and frolic together. Rambunctious and playful, they wrestle, cuff each other on the head, body-surf in the current, and play other bear games.

Male and female bears come together repeatedly to mate during the one- to two-week interval during the spring when the females are in estrus. Females with cubs that are less than two to three years old do not generally mate. During the mating season, aggressive encounters between adult males are more frequent as they compete to mate.

Brown bears also form feeding aggregations in which

the bears share a common food source, such as a carcass or a salmon stream. For a few weeks each summer when the salmon are running, bears aggregate along the streams of Katmai. During the peak of the sockeye run in mid-July, up to 12 to 15 bears might fish at Brooks Falls vicinity at one time, vying for a share of the thousands of salmon that fight their way up Brooks River each day.

Communication between brown bears can be complex. They do not appear to have highly ritualized forms of communication as do many of the more social mammal species, such as wolves. Rather, their interactions seem to depend on behavioral signals, such as body position, eye contact, and vocalizations. These signals largely represent a language of aggression and submission.

Brown bears seem to define a loose social ranking according to age and sex in which adult males are typically dominant, adult females with cubs are next. Younger adults, both male and female, follow. Subadults and adolescent bears come last. A bear's behavior reflects its sex and age class, but, perhaps even more, it reflects the bear's personality.

Females with cubs are the most cautious and defensive of bears. They are the only class of bears to consistently challenge adult males and will defend their young against any perceived threat. The younger the cubs are, the more aggressive will be a mother's behavior in protecting them.

Large boars sometimes attack and eat young cubs. If a large boar approaches her cubs, a sow will usually challenge him. Females may alter their fishing patterns drastically when they have cubs, avoiding crowded areas where the young bears may be endangered, even if the fishing there is exceptional.

When two bears have an aggressive encounter, both usually issue a challenge threat simultaneously, approaching or charging the other with head raised and mouth open. They may growl or roar; the louder the roar, the more serious the challenge. These threats are almost always bluffs. The subordinate bear indicates its submission by gradually easing off by lowering its head, looking away, or sitting down. A dominant bear may defuse an aggressive situation by exposing its neck or walking away, indicating that it does not intend to fight.

Forms of Brown Bear Interaction
Near Salmon Streams

Avoidance —of a dominant bear by a subordinate bear is the most common defensive behavior.

Head-low Threat —The head is held low with ears laid back, body orientation varies, and low monotone roaring accompanies a slowly opening and closing mouth. The distance between bears is generally less than about 12 feet (four meters).

Head-high Threat —In this more intense threat, one or both bears extend their heads diagonally upward toward the opponent, orient their bodies frontally, and roar loudly and continuously from open mouths. They shift their weight to the hind legs, presumably to free the front legs for striking, and stand very close to each other.

Charges—occur in several forms. A direct charge is a hard, fast rush at an opponent accompanied by low growling that increases to a loud roar. A short charge is similar to the early phase of a direct charge except that it is halted after three or four strides. A third type of charge seems to involve a combination of threat and avoidance behavior with one bear performing exaggerated rocking and hopping movements toward another bear.

Contact —includes striking and biting. Strikes are typically oriented toward the chest and shoulders, while biting is directed at the head and neck.

Amicable —interactions are brief encounters where two bears paw, mouth, rub, or otherwise interact in a non-antagonistic manner.

Play —is more prolonged than amicable interaction and is distinguished from antagonistic behavior by exaggerated head movements, lack of loud growling, and restrained striking and biting.

(after Egbert and Stokes, 1974, based on observations at McNeil River, Alaska)

A subordinate bear is usually not allowed to walk away from an encounter. If it does, it could be attacked by the dominant bear, which sees this behavior as a challenge to its dominance. However, no exact rules govern bear behavior. Each bear responds differently according to its sex, age, personality, family status, and mood.

A Season to Spawn

Due to the physiological changes brought on by the return to freshwater, the sockeye salmon will have ceased eating by the time they reach Brooks Falls. The fish that make it beyond the falls will continue up into Brooks Lake, becoming redder with every passing day, their backs humping up and their jaws hooking over. Navigating by its sense of smell, each salmon finds the mouth of the creek where it was spawned. Thousands of salmon churn the lake water at the mouths of feeder creeks, waiting for the biological cue to continue up the narrow waterway.

When the eggs in a female ripen and separate, and a male's sperm is mature, the fish embark up the streams. As they approach the spawning grounds, the males become increasingly aggressive. They attack other mature males as well as jacks, males that are not fully mature but are sexually precocious.

The males are alert for females preparing to spawn. When a female is ready, she swims slowly near the spawning ground as she chooses a location to dig her nest, or redd. Digging the nest is the first step in the mating sequence, which lasts for several hours. The female turns on her side and slaps the river bottom with her tail, whisking gravel downstream. She does this repeatedly, using the stream current to help move the gravel. As she digs, the dominant male draws alongside her, quivering, and crosses over her back from side to side. She continues hitting the bottom, probing the nest depth with her anal fin, until the 16- to 18-inch diameter hole reaches a depth of at least a foot.

Whenever the female probes the depth, the male swims beside her in anticipation of spawning. When the female decides the nest is deep enough, she positions herself over it. The male lines up next to the female and both fish pulsate over the redd, mouths agape and fins vibrating. At

the same instant, they release eggs and milt into the current.

Other males and jacks may rush in to join the pair at the last moment, releasing their milt at the instant of spawning. The sperm swim directly into the eggs, fertilizing 98 percent of them as they sink to the bottom.

Immediately after spawning, the female begins covering the eggs with gravel. She beats the streambed upstream of the nest, first covering the just-laid eggs, then slapping the gravel to dig a second nest. This sequence is repeated three more times as the male and female spawn, laying 500 to 1,000 eggs each time.

By the time the spawning is completed, the female's tail

Bears at Brooks Falls observe each other warily. The dominant male is to be avoided.
JAMES GAVIN

is shredded from beating it on the river bottom to dig the redds and cover the eggs. With all of her remaining strength, she hovers near the nests, guarding them until she can no longer resist the current and drifts downstream to die.

Sockeyes usually die about nine days after they begin spawning. Dead salmon flood downstream, settle on the bottom, wash up on shore, and choke the streams that hold their fertilized eggs. The nutrients in their decaying bodies are scavenged by gulls, foxes, and bears.

From the Gravel to the Sea

Within an hour after coming to rest on the gravel river bottom, the salmon eggs begin to harden, the first step in the process of ripening into fry. As the embryo develops, its demand for oxygen grows until, finally, it must break through the egg membrane. Sometime in February, a tiny alevin creeps from the egg into the dark spaces between the gravel of the streambed. It worms its way through the river bottom, yolk hanging from its belly, avoiding the light of the free-running stream. The alevin won't emerge from the dark crevices in the gravel until the yolk is used up. Then it swims upward into the flowing water of the stream, gulping air to inflate its swim bladder and becomes buoyant for the first time.

In the spring, the tiny sockeye, now called a fry, descend to the lake or stream where they will feed on plankton for one to three years, the longest freshwater stay of any Pacific salmon fry. Only 10 to 20 percent of the fry will survive to swim into the ocean. The rest will be eaten by Arctic char, Dolly Varden, osprey, gulls, and other birds and fish.

In the late fall, the young fry metamorphose in the cooling water; their skin changes from a dull barred appearance to a shiny silver. Their physiological processes change to allow them to live in salt water. These transformed fry,

Dead salmon become food for scavengers such as ravens and gulls. Nothing is wasted.

JAMES GAVIN

Each brown bear develops an individual fishing style and technique. JAMES GAVIN

ing on plankton, invertebrates, fish and crustaceans.

As they mature in the ocean, they may be eaten by larger fish or be captured by high seas driftnet fishing fleets. Salmon face increasing stresses throughout the cycle of their lives, including pollution from logging and other industries, physical barriers such as dams, and over-fishing.

After two to three years circulating in the Pacific, the Bristol Bay sockeye salmon begin the long journey back to the freshwater stream where they were born. The fish show incredible endurance during their homing odyssey. They may swim 24 hours and travel up to 30 miles (50 kilometers) a day during their final swim to freshwater.

When they reach freshwater, they undergo physiological changes as their bodies prepare for spawning: they stop eating, they become red, their jaws hook over, and their flesh softens. Then the salmon swim upstream to their spawning ground, the final leg of their journey.

now called smolts, remain in the cold lake water through the winter. Some of them depart for the sea in the lengthening days of spring. When the water on the surface of the lake warms in early summer, any smolts that have not migrated to the ocean will revert to their dull appearance and remain in freshwater for another year.

When the smolts reach the Pacific, they are juvenile salmon. They swim in a huge zone that encloses an area of approximatel two million square miles (five million square kilometers). Bristol Bay sockeye range as far south as California and east nearly to the Kamchatka Peninsula in the Soviet Union.

The sockeye circulate with seven species of salmon from around the Pacific rim, feed-

One Pound Bears

In summer, the lives of brown bears are driven by the need to eat and store fat. The survival of both the individual and the species depends on it. Katmai bears feast on fresh red salmon meat throughout the long summer days of the fish run. They consume up to ten or more fish a day, then wander off to nap in the tall, waving grass.

Brown bears are food opportunists, ingesting whatever nutrition is available. Carnivores by evolution, they have re-adapted to become plant eaters with powerful jaws and sturdy molars that grind and pulverize. They amble through the woods and bogs, feeding on tubers, roots, insects and berries. The long, curving claws and the massive shoulder muscles that form their humps are designed to dig plants and animals from the earth.

Perhaps a bear's most important food-finding tool is its nose. Just as our world is dominated by visual images, a bear's world is dominated by odors. They rely on their noses to identify everything and to locate food. Bears can even track animals by the scent of their footprints. Combined with their ability to eat almost any food, their powerful noses enable them to survive in a wide range of natural habitats.

After mating in the spring, the sow gains up to forty percent of her fall weight, enough to sustain the cubs during the winter by incubation and nursing. The fertilized eggs do not implant in her uterus until after she enters the den in late fall. If she has not eaten enough, the eggs will not implant.

In the dark warmth of the winter den, a sleeping sow gives birth to two or three tiny hairless cubs. Each cub weighs less than one pound at birth.

They continue their development in the den, which is practically an extension of the mother's womb. They nurse on their sleeping mother throughout the winter, gaining weight and strength. One day, the sow will awaken and push her way out of the den into the spring sunshine with furry cubs tumbling behind her.

The Woman Who Married a Bear

Native people, from the Gwich'in Indians of northern Alaska to the Ainu of Japan, have traditionally addressed bears with titles of intimacy and respect. Grandfather, Grandmother, Sister, Brother, Husband: these were names for brown bear. The people believed that bears possessed great power; they traced their own origins back with the bears. The story of the woman who married a bear, told widely in Native communities throughout North America, describes the delicate relationship between humans and bears that has existed for centuries.

A young woman was out picking berries in the mountains one day. She met a man on the trail who was kind and friendly. He asked her to go with him, and so she did. They lived together eating berries and squirrels in the tundra. When it became cold, he dug a cave in the side of the mountain. The woman liked living with the man and forgot where her home had been. They went into the cave to live. The woman liked the man very much but she suspected he was a bear. When he was with her he seemed like a man, but when he dug squirrels from the earth or hunted he looked like a bear. She gave birth to two children in the den that winter.

In the spring, her brothers went bear hunting, as they did every spring. That year, they came to the den of their sister and her husband. The bear-man went to see why dogs were barking outside the den. Before he went outside the den, he sang his wife a song. He told her how to sing and burn the head of a hunted bear. Then he went outside and the woman's brothers killed him.

She took her two children and went to live with her family again. She taught the people in the village how to sing and burn the head of a hunted bear. She told them how to behave around bears and how to address them with respect. She lived with her family, but every day her body grew more hairy. One day her brothers taunted her. She turned into a bear and tore the whole family, even her mother, to shreds.

Gary Snyder, in his book *The Practice of the Wild* wrote the following words about the story of the woman who married a bear.

The young woman and her

children are irrevocably bears now: the human world will not accept them. They must return to the wilderness, having accomplished their task — to teach humans the precise manners in regard to bears. Perhaps all this was planned by the Bear Fathers and Mothers, who chose an intrepid young male to be the messenger. For each of the actors there was a price: the bear and the woman's family lost their lives. One cannot cross between realms without paying a high price. She lost her lover and her humanity to become a bear with two rowdy cubs alone in the wild.

That was very long ago. After that time human beings had good relations with the bears. Around the top of the world many peoples have hunted and celebrated and feasted with the bears outdoors in the snow every year in midwinter. Bears and people have shared the berryfields and the salmon streams without much trouble summer after summer. Bears have been careful not to hunt and kill humans as prey, although they would fight back when attacked.

But that period is over now. The bears are being killed, the humans are everywhere, and the green world is being unraveled and shredded and burned by the spreading of a gray world that seems to have no end. If it weren't for a few old people from the time before, we wouldn't even know this tale.

> Despite the heavy odds against their survival, about 75,000 to 100,000 salmon make it past Brooks Falls to spawn in Brooks Lake and nearby streams every year. GARY LACKIE

[1] Excerpted from *The Practice of the Wild*, © 1990 by Gary Snyder, pp. 168-169. Published by North Point Press and reprinted by permission.

Cliffs more than 100 feet high have been carved in the ashfall of the Valley of Ten Thousand Smokes. NATIONAL PARK SERVICE PHOTO BY ROBERT BELOUS

CHAPTER 3

The Land They Found

In the beginning there was water over all the earth, and it was very cold; the water was covered with ice, and there were no people. Then the ice ground together, making long ridges and hummocks. At this time came a man from the far side of the great water and stopped on the ice hills near where Pikmiktalik now is, taking for his wife a she-wolf. By and by he had many children, which were always born in pairs—a boy and a girl. Each pair spoke a tongue of their own, different from that of their parents and different from any spoken by their brothers and sisters.

As soon as they were large enough each pair was sent out in a different direction from the others, and thus the family spread far and near from the ice hills, which now became snow-covered mountains. As the snow melted it ran down the hillsides, scooping out ravines and river beds, and so making the earth with its streams.

The twins peopled the earth with their children, and as each pair with their children spoke a language different from the others, the various tongues found on the earth were established and continue until this day.

Edward William Nelson [1]

---

[1] Reprinted by permission of the Smithsonian Institution Press from "The Eskimo about Bering Strait," by Edward William Nelson, from <u>Bureau of American Ethnology, 18</u>. Smithsonian Institution 1899. p. 482.

Walking to Alaska

The first residents of Katmai may have walked to get there, coming by way of Beringia, a land mass to the north now submerged beneath the Bering Sea. During the peak of the last great Ice Age, beginning some 25,000 to 18,000 years ago, Beringia was free of the massive glaciers that occupied the stony highlands to the west. The ice sheets and glaciers that cloaked much of North America locked up enough water to maintain the level of the sea about 1000 feet (300 meters) lower than its current level.

Beringia connected Asia and North America as one great continent. It extended as far south as the Pribilof Islands and the Alaska Peninsula. Bristol Bay sat high and dry above the sea and the Alaska Peninsula was not a peninsula.

Although we call it the Bering land bridge, the people who lived there did not think of it as a bridge — this land mass was more than 1000 miles (1,600 kilometers) wide.

Scientists have developed several scenarios for the nature of Beringia using information from the pollen record, fossil plants, and relic plant communities. The evidence suggests that the landscape was likely a combination of tundra and steppe, and supported healthy populations of large herbivores. It was a vast rolling plain with sand dunes and expanses of sagebrush, grasses and sedge.

Wooly mammoths, which had giant curving tusks and long auburn hair, roamed there, as did caribou, horses and saiga antelope. Seals and beluga whales swam in the fertile seas along Beringia's southern coast and waterfowl flocked in the estuaries and salt marshes.

Archaeologists believe that people probably lived in isolated groups and hunted the large mammals. However, much land where evidence of human settlements in Beringia might be found is submerged beneath the sea.

The Ice Age abated around 12,000 years ago when the earth's climate warmed and the glaciers began to melt. As the weight of the ice was removed, the earth's crust actually rebounded, much like a balloon held under water that springs up when released. The upward movement of the rebounding crust helped the meltwater to drain from the highlands. Water spilled across the rolling coastal dunes from the melting glaciers and huge deltas formed. The Yukon River extended 500 miles farther than it does today, nearly to Siberia, as it drained meltwater from the glaciers of the Alaska Range. The sea level rose several feet in one human lifetime. Finally the Bering Sea and the Arctic Ocean joined to form the Bering Strait, and Beringia was submerged.

As the glaciers receded, they left a rolling landscape with hunks of ice and rock and freshly ground soil heaped on the frozen earth. Shallow ponds sparkled on the raw moraines, prevented from draining into the soil by ice and clay deposits. Vast wetland areas remained in the wake of the glaciers, colonized first by scrub willow and peat moss.

The Ice Age in Katmai

What was Katmai like during this period? When hunters stalked wooly mammoth on the plains of Beringia, nearly all of Katmai was buried under ice. The glaciers that flowed from the Aleutian Range blanketed and gouged the land that would become Naknek Lake, Brooks Lake, Grosvenor Lake and Lake Coville. Farther north, Kulik, Nonvianuk and Iliamna Lakes were also buried under ice.

Like melting snowpiles in the springtime, the glaciers dumped mounds of rock and soil at their edges as the ice melted away. These mounds, or moraines, contained any and all materials that happened to be there, in no particular order. Giant boulders, fine silt, blocks of ice, gravels and clay: these are the materials of moraine. Terminal moraines mark the outermost reach of the glaciers at the height of the late Wisconsin Ice Age. As the glaciers retreated, moraines dammed the meltwater in an enormous lake encompassing all of today's Brooks-Naknek-Grosvenor-Coville lake system.

The glaciers retreated in four stages (or stades) during this most recent, the Brooks Lake, glaciation. Nature's road signs, terminal moraines mark the progress of the retreat. During the second retreat stage (Iliamna Stade), the ice margin followed the western shores of Naknek, Becharof and Nonvianuk Lakes. The moraines deposited on the western shores of

The seldom-visited Katmai coast. L. SUMNER

these lakes dammed the meltwater from the retreating glaciers, forming the lakes. As the glaciers retreated farther (Newhalen and Iliuk Stades), they stopped for a geologic moment on top of present day Kulik Lake, Grosvenor Lake and Iliuk Arm, dumping the moraines which separate Iliuk Arm from Naknek and Brooks Lakes, Grosvenor from Coville Lake, and Nonvianuk from Kulik Lake.

Peat bogs and scrubby birch forests sprang up almost immediately on top of the newly exposed soils of the moraines. To determine the age of the moraines, scientists collected the oldest peat from the bottom of the soil column. These samples represent the first peat bogs that colonized the moraines. Radiocarbon measurements indicate the moraines are approximately 9,000 years old.

Lake levels dropped as the glaciers retreated into the mountains but held steady long enough to develop stable shorelines. These "fossil" shorelines appear as lake terraces around and above the present day lakes. Naknek Lake is ringed by three lake terraces, the highest of which is nearly 100 feet (30 meters) above the present lake level. Eventually the lakes breached the morainal dams that held them, and water coursed across the lowlands.

At first, the rivers downcut rapidly through the loose silt and gravel deposits. As the water levels equalized and the gradient decreased, the rivers slowed and took on the meandering aspect they have today.

When the lake levels dropped, so too did the river levels. Terraces along the Brooks and other rivers mark former streambanks. The trail to Brooks Falls and the road to Brooks Lake cross several river terraces.

The Brooks Camp area began to emerge from the glacial lakes about 10,000 years ago as the level of Naknek Lake dropped. The glacier occupying Iliuk Arm deposited an outwash plain between Naknek and Brooks Lakes. As Naknek Lake drained, the Brooks River eroded the outwash.

One day a bedrock scarp appeared in the dropping river, the first appearance of the waterfall we know today as Brooks Falls. Deposits on the south side of the river are beach deposits from an older path of Brooks River; farther south lie the outwash deposits breached by the river thousands of years ago. These glacial deposits in the Brooks Camp area are capped by eight-to-ten inches of creamy-colored ash from the 1912 eruption of Novarupta.

North to Alaska: Subduction and the Aleutian Island Chain

If the rocks could tell their own story, they would speak of movement and change. Katmai sits near the boundary of two tectonic plates, the Pacific Plate and the North American Plate. The plates are slabs of the earth's crust that glide over its surface. New crust is produced at spreading centers on the ocean floor, and crust is recirculated into the earth's interior at subduction zones. A subduction zone lies beneath Katmai.

Ever since the breakup of the supercontinent Pangaea some 240 million years ago, the Pacific Plate has moved north. Its current rate of movement is about 2-1/4 inches (six centimeters) per year. More dense than continental crust, oceanic crust of the Pacific Plate plunges beneath the North American Plate. As the Pacific Plate dives into the earth's interior, the tremendous heat and pressure melts it, freeing masses of buoyant molten rock to stream upward

Glacial Features and Related Landforms

Till —Till is the haphazard pile of densely packed rock, gravel and other deposits dropped directly from the glacial ice. Till includes everything from house-sized or larger boulders (called erratics) to finely powdered rock "flour", to vegetation and ice.

Terminal (End) Moraine—Generally speaking, where till is the deposit, moraine is the landform. Terminal moraines mark the location of former glacier margins where the retreating glacier maintained a stable position for a period of time. Glaciers form several other types of moraines such as lateral (side) moraines, medial moraines at the confluence of two glaciers, ground moraine, and others.

Eskers —are ridges formed by deposits from mini-rivers that carve their way down through the glacier ice. Meandering down the length of the glacier, the surface expression of an esker is like a giant mole trail, flat on top and raised above the level of the surrounding ground surface. While not evident in Katmai, eskers are found in other parts of Alaska as well as New England and the Midwest.

Kames —may be cone shaped or simply piles, but are usually stratified. Formed where the streams on a glacier deposit sediment into a hole or crevasse, kames take a variety of forms when the glacier disappears and only the piles are left.

Pitted outwash —Pitted outwash occurs where wasting glacial ice is lodged in outwash or other sediments. As the ice melts, the sediments collapse to form pits.

Lake Terraces—mark former shorelines. Deposited at the lake shoreline when waters were higher, lake terraces are underlain by coarse deposits or fine-grained lake sediment, such as you might find on the different types of modern day beaches.

Outwash —As its name implies, outwash is the sand and gravel carried from the front of a glacier by the meltwater flowing away. It forms relatively flat plains of sand and gravel in front of moraines, and the particles may sort themselves according to grain size by falling out of suspension to match the force of the water.

Drumlins —Sausage-shaped hills oriented parallel to the flow direction of a glacier, drumlins form when a glacier overrides a moraine or hill and reworks the deposits.

Abandoned Channel Deposits—Former stream beds lace the lowlands in Katmai; you'll see them from any airplane flight you take in the park. These unsorted sand and gravel deposits meander in front of the old moraines which they used to drain, or along the sides of mountains where waters flowed next to mountain glaciers.

toward the surface. This molten rock, or magma, may migrate to the surface, erupting to form volcanos. Other magma may stop before it reaches the surface, cooling at depth to form crystalline igneous rock bodies, or batholiths.

Most of the volcanos in Alaska are part of the Aleutian Volcanic Arc, a chain of 80 volcanos that stretches more than 1200 miles (1900 kilometers) from Cook Inlet to Siberia. These volcanos were created as a result of the underlying subduction zone. Many of the Aleutian volcanos are still alive, with Mount Redoubt, Mount Augustine and Westdahl Volcano being the most recently active.

The Pacific Plate wrinkled and fractured the early Alaskan continental crust as if it were pushing a tablecloth across a table. Folds, faults and basins developed within the crust of the North American Plate. The mountains shed sediments into offshore basins formed by crustal warping. These deposits eventually lithified to produce thick sequences of sedimentary rocks.

Later, the rocks in Katmai ruptured along a fault almost parallel to the coast, the Bruin Bay Fault. The landward side moved up while the seaward side dropped down in response to the enormous compressive forces.

This major fault runs between Mount Katolinat and Mount La Gorce; it follows

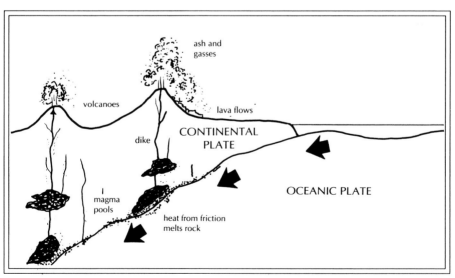

Generalized subduction zone

Contact Creek, cuts Grosvenor Lake in half, and touches the southeast end of Kulik Lake. The uplands on the northwest side of the fault eroded, exposing batholiths and the rocks in which they were emplaced. To the south, in Becharof National Wildlife Refuge, two unique volcanic features, the Ukinrek Maars and Gas Rocks, occur atop the Bruin Bay Fault.

Splinters of crust, called terranes, or microcontinents, moved north with the Pacific Plate, piggy-back fashion. As the Pacific Plate moved beneath the North American Plate, the terranes were, in a fashion, scraped off. Eventually, as many as 50 terranes reached and adhered to the coast of Alaska. Most of south and southeast coastal Alaska is a patchwork of these accreted terranes arranged in broad bands that roughly follow the coastline. Major faults mark their borders, juxtaposing wildly different rock units next to one another. One such fault, the Border Ranges Fault, slices between Katmai and Kodiak. The Border Ranges Fault follows the northwest edge of Kodiak Island and traces a line across Cook Inlet to touch Homer and south Anchorage.

Katmai is part of the Peninsular Terrane, which is composed of Jurassic sedimentary rocks that have been intruded by batholiths. Kodiak is primarily Chugach Terrane, offshore mudslide deposits, known as flysch, which were deposited during the Cretaceous Period.

Katmai remains geologically active as seen in the 1953 eruption of Trident. U.S. NAVY

Geologic Units in Katmai

The Cottonwood Bay Greenstone (Late Triassic) which includes submarine lava flows, chert, and sills, is the oldest rock unit in Katmai. In Katmai it forms pendants or caps over the Alaska-Aleutian Ranges batholith and has been almost entirely metamorphosed to greenschist.

The Talkeetna Formation (Early Jurassic) consists of volcanic deposits interbedded with siltstone, sandstone, and conglomerate. The Talkeetna Formation and all older rocks are intruded by plutonic rocks of the Alaska-Aleutian Ranges batholith. The Talkeetna Formation is exposed on Dumpling Mountain.

The Naknek Formation (Late Jurassic) consists of siltstone, conglomerate, and sandstone formed as the uplands eroded and fine sediment and cobbles were deposited in offshore basins, shallow seas, and river bottoms. The Naknek Formation is the most widespread rock unity in Katmai. Mount Katolinat, the Buttress Ranges, and the non-volcanic mountains in the Valley of Ten Thousand Smokes are composed of rocks of the Naknek Formation. A conglomerate unit of the Naknek can be seen along the Ukak River trail that descends from the Three Forks Overlook.

The Kaguyak Formation (Upper Cretaceous) overlies all older strata in the Katmai area. It consists of sandstone, siltstone, and thin limestone beds. Depositional features indicate it was deposited as submarine mudslides in a deep marine basin.

The Alaska-Aleutian Ranges Batholith (Jurassic and Tertiary) was formed as great masses of molten rock rose up toward the earth's surface, embedding in the Naknek Formation and other older rocks. The batholith formation stretches all the way to Denali Park and is exposed on the northwest side of the Bruin Bay Fault on mountains such as Mount Kelez and Mount LaGorce.

The Meshik Volcanic Arc (Middle Tertiary) the oldest volcanos in Katmai, now extinct, erupted some 40 million years ago. The unit also includes intrusive rocks and extends from the southern Alaska Peninsula beyond Katmai to Iliamna. In Katmai, it outcrops north of Naknek and Grosvenor Lakes.

Recent Volcanic Units (Tertiary and Quaternary) include central vent deposits, lava flows, ash flows, pumice, ash falls, breccias, and other deposits and rocks from modern volcanos such as Novarupta, Trident Volcano, Mount Mageik, and Mount Griggs.

CHAPTER 4

Beings of the Land

The Grand Mosaic

We packed ourselves and our pile of gear into a Cessna and followed the lakes north from Brooks Camp. The plane rounded the point that jutted toward Brooks Campground from Mount La Gorce, and climbed east over Bay of Islands, flying over Lake Grosvenor, American Creek, and beyond.

A pattern stretched below the wings and I stared down at the soft green mosaic trying to discern an order. Ancient winding riverbeds stood forth below us like finger tracings on a now-dry window. Pale green reindeer lichen capped the low hills daubed at wide

Caribou. HAROLD WILSON

intervals with spruce. Dark green bands of alder fingered up the creeks from the shorelines of the lakes to higher lands, giving way to rocky tundra.

The pattern is movement. The glaciers reach down from the mountains like a hand extended and pulled back, extended and pulled back. The glaciers and greenery tango to this game, waters and vegetation dance across the hills, twirling and spinning together. Over time, the plants flow through the valleys like water, the branches of the rivers sway like trees in the wind. Seasons and years flash through the dance like a strobe, each moment a logical result of all that passed before.

Major shifts in plant communities arise, not unlike the

course of a human life, from seemingly subtle changes in conditions. So unique is each plant in its specialization that differences in sunlight, moisture, soil, or elevation give advantage to entirely different sets of plants. English lacks a suitable word for the marvelous entities we call ecosystems. These thriving near-creatures formed of shrubs, moss, wildflowers, lichen, soils, insects, water, and a miraculous melange of other beings and moments deserve a name as pungent and vigorous as they are. Fortunately, the names for the individual ecosystems are more richly organic, imparted by people who spent their lives as members of the communities.

Boreal forest: from the Latin borealis, of or pertaining to the north wind (Boreas, Greek god of the North Wind). Forest, from the Old French, means the outside wood, the wood lying outside the walls of the park. Boreal Forest is also called Taiga, from the Russian word for "land of the little sticks." Tundra is also from the Russian. Bog, from the Irish and Gaelic bogach, means soft, to bend. Muskeg was named by the Cree and Ojibwa Indians of Canada.

Above Treeline

From afar, the mountains look soft, like the velveted antlers of caribou in summer. The trees have not climbed the gentle peaks, halted by a combination of temperature, latitude and elevation. With tree line at 1500 to 2000 feet, much of Katmai is alpine tundra, sometimes spacious and airy, sometimes desolate and windtorn.

Alpine tundra is inhospitable for most of the year. Howling winds, freezing temperatures, scanty soil, and a short growing season are the conditions plants and animals must endure.

Plants adapted to this environment develop extensive creeping root systems and keep their above-ground body small. Moss campion and other plants form mats, dense clusters which afford protection in the wind and help develop and anchor soil.

Many species are evergreen, enabling them to photosynthesize early and utilize their limited energy for seed and flower production. Alpine plants are vigorously active during the short summer.

Summer in the tundra is exquisite. The joy of renewal

floods across the wide expanses. The rocks seem to vibrate with the heat of life radiating from the earth.

Dwarf willows cling to the ground, exposing their catkins between lichen encrusted rocks; delicate wildflowers glow with color—fuchsia Kamchatka rhododendron, deep-aqua glaucous gentian, pale-yellow lousewort, hot-pink dwarf fireweed, creamy saxifrage, mauve rosecrown, white heather, deep green heath...

Arctic ground squirrels scamper across the rocks, feeding on the sparse vegetation, occasionally darting out of their tunnels to scold a snow bunting. Bands of caribou wander across the high plateaus and snow fields, feasting on willow and dwarf birch, grasses and sedges. They move

The land above treeline.
JEAN BODEAU

quickly, flowing across the tundra. This is the time to fatten; caribou bulls will add several inches to their back and rump in preparation for rutting season. At that time, they stop eating, not resuming until the rut is over several weeks later.

August. Darkness lingers a few minutes longer each night. On some mornings, a damp chill hangs in the sunshine, quickly dispelled but not forgotten. Autumn creeps across the tundra, barely noticeable at first—a few golden willow leaves, mountain avens turned wispy cotton, a deep reddish tint on the bearberry leaves. Blueberries dot the shrubs. Bright berries such as crowberry, bearberry, cranberry (both lowbush and high) enclose the well-tended seeds, fruits of the summer's flowers. Their carbohydrates and simple sugars nourish squirrels, birds, brown bears and humans, who in turn, disperse the seeds.

Now autumn flames across the tundra. Vibrant red, luminous yellow and enduring evergreen ignite the frosty landscape with color. The land itself, the whole of the tundra, is fertile, energetic and giving.

As fall passes into winter, the male caribou become increasingly restless. They spar frequently with the other bulls, brandishing their antlers now shed of velvet. They approach the females, nuzzling, sniffing, licking — waiting for the hormonal trigger of estrus. The bulls fight with each other for dominance. Rituals between males and females become more elaborate and frenzied as the time for mating draws near. As the females move one by one into heat, each is approached by a bull, whose dominance has by now been proven, and they mate.

When the caribou have finished mating, usually by the end of October, the males shed their antlers and begin browsing once again. The females retain their antlers through the winter. They are the only females in the deer family to grow antlers. Pawing through the snow with their broad hooves, caribou feed on lichen and sedge through the long winter.

Other animals remain active during the winter too. Small animals such as voles and shrews develop trail systems beneath the snow to reach frozen vegetation in this warm protected environment. Red foxes will follow and excavate these trails, catching voles as a staple of their winter diet. Nomadic ptarmigan feed on the buds and twigs of birch and willow.

The marmots, true hibernators, sleep in their burrows until spring.

When winter days lengthen, pregnant caribou cows lead the migration to the calving grounds. Caribou herds return to their calving grounds year after year to birth the calves conceived during the fall rut. Calves from the previous year accompany their mothers, imprinting the location of the calving ground in their memories.

Each pregnant cow, if she has eaten enough during the

A Few Mat-Forming Shrubs

Starry cassiope *(Cassiope stelleriana)*

Tiny, alternate leaves line the stems of this low, trailing, evergreen shrub that forms mats two to four inches high with one bell-shaped white to pink flower per stalk. Prefers protected slopes, snow deposition areas, and moist seepage areas.

White mountain avens *(Dryas octopetala)*

Small herbaceous evergreen dwarf shrub with solitary, white, eight-petaled flowers; grows close to the ground in rocky riverbeds and alpine tundra, seeds become feathery in July through August.

Crowberry (mossberry, blackberry) *(Empetrum nigrum)*

Creeping, evergreen, heatherlike shrub grows to six inches in most environments in Katmai and is one of most common species in heath mats. Dark purple, juicy berries are ripe in August, last beneath the snow throughout the winter and are eaten extensively by brown bears.

Twinflower *(Linnaea borealis)*

Creeping evergreen dwarf shrub, or herbaceous, to four inches, with rounded or elliptic opposite leaves and paired white fragrant flowers.

Alpine azalea *(Loiseleuria procumbens)*

A trailing, evergreen subshrub, it grows in mats to two inches in dry rocky tundra. Small, leathery, elliptic leaves are shiny on top, rolled under with white hairs beneath, 1/4-inch long and 1/16-inch wide. Bell-shaped pink or white flowers from May through July.

Luetkea/Alaska spirea *(Luetkea pectinata)*

Leutkea is a small (two- to six in.), creeping shrub common in alpine tundra where it forms mats. Racemes of small white flowers bloom all summer on the tops of stalks with clusters of long forked leaves at the base.

Aleutian mountain heath *(Phyllodoce aleutica)*

Five to 15 yellow-green bell shaped flowers on top of two- to six-inch evergreen plants bloom from June through late August. The small leaves resemble needles. Forms pure mats several yards in diameter in protected depressions and adjacent to snow.

winter, will bear one calf. When she does, she will chase the yearling away, devoting her full attention to the new calf. She must be alert at all times, watching for the wolves and bears that depend on caribou and moose calves as easy spring prey. Wolves and bears also take caribou left weakened by winter.

The two caribou herds that live in Katmai, the Mulchatna and the Northern Alaska Peninsula herds, migrate across small areas compared to the ranges of large herds in interior Alaska. The Mulchatna herd ranges north of the Naknek River to Lake Iliamna and beyond. Its calving ground north of Lake Iliamna is typically between Turquoise and Twin Lakes in Lake Clark National Park. The Northern Alaska Peninsula herd has drifted north from its historic range between Port Moller and the Naknek River to mingle with the Mulchatna herd. The Northern Alaska Peninsula herd calves north of Port Heiden.

Forest of the North Wind

As the glaciers retreated from the lowlands and the first people arrived in Katmai, spruce spread from south central Alaska, arriving on the Alaska Peninsula about 6,000 years ago. The arrival of this tree as the climate warmed changed the character of Alaska and most of northern North America. It quickly spread and became the dominant tree in the boreal forests. It diversified and adapted to the range of conditions it found in the wake of the glaciers.

The tall, hardy white spruce thrived on the sun-warmed slopes facing south, and on well-drained soils. It was joined by paper birch and towering balsam poplar. Black spruce, a poor competitor with the vigorous white spruce, was forced into the poorly drained and colder areas, which were frequently underlain by permafrost. In moist coastal areas extending down to Canada and the northwestern United States, towering Sitka spruce and western hemlock dominated.

Along with the spruce, alder and birch also sprang up as the boreal forest extended rapidly across the continent,

Spruce in Katmai

White spruce *(Picea glauca)*

White spruce is the most important tree in spruce-birch forest and prefers well-drained and sandy soils. It grows mostly in open forests in association with paper birch but is seldom found where permafrost is close to the surface.

Height is the easiest way to distinguish between the medium to tall white spruce and the small- to medium black spruce. White spruce needles are longer than 1/2 inch and sharp. Black spruce needles are typically shorter and blunter; white spruce twigs lack the hair that characterize black spruce.

Black spruce *(Picea mariana)*

Black spruce tends to grow in cold wet flats, boggy areas, north-facing slopes and silty valley bottoms.

Sitka spruce *(Picea sitchensis)*

Sitka spruce is a tree of the coastal forest and is at the western limit of its range in Katmai. A large tree, known to grow to 225 feet tall and eight feet in diameter, it is heavily logged in southeast Alaska. Sitka spruce needles are flattened, up to an inch long and have two whitish bands of stomata on their lower surfaces.

an expansion that continues today. The Harriman Expedition stopped in Kukak Bay on the outer Katmai coast during their explorations through Alaska in 1899. They found fossilized spruce, alder, and birch, as well as maple and even Sequoia.

Katmai, which is situated at the transition zone between the interior, the Gulf of Alaska coast, and the Aleutians, marks the range limit of all three spruce found there. White and black spruce, trees of the interior, reach their southwestern limit on the Alaska Peninsula. Sitka spruce is the great giant of the coastal forest, and lives no further west than the Katmai coast.

Beneath the canopy of the dominant trees in a forest lives the understory, a shorter forest often more diverse than the trees above it. In the white spruce-birch forest, moss and low shrubs thrive on cool moist slopes. Grasses prefer the dry slopes, and willow, alder and dwarf birch are found in high open forests near timberline.

Other species of the white spruce forest include high bush cranberry, fireweed, milk vetch, pyrola, bluejoint grass, horsetail, and clubmoss. Brooks Camp and the lower portion of the Dumpling Mountain trail are in white spruce-birch forest. Wildflowers commonly seen in these areas include wild geranium, northern bedstraw, Jacob's ladder and yarrow.

The understory of a black spruce forest is often a wet tundra or wetland environment.

Moose

Moose fill a similar niche in the forest as caribou do in the tundra. A long-legged herbivore, the Alaska moose is the largest member of the deer family worldwide. Males typically weigh 1,200 to 1,500 pounds; females reach 1,300 pounds.

To maintain their huge bodies, moose browse almost continuously on willow, birch, and poplar twigs. Tender sedge and horsetail shoots round out their diet in the spring. Moose eat practically anything that photosynthesizes, and water is no barrier to their feasting. In the summer, moose wade across lakes and ponds, their heads submerged as they pluck the succulent pond weeds from the bottom.

In the fall, when the mountain ash berries have turned a brilliant red and the fireweed has burst into cotton, the males begin to scrape their massive racks against trees. The velvet drops off in bloody clumps, and moose prepare for the rut. The bulls stop eating and battle for the privilege of mating with the cows. They bellow through the forest, aggressive, driven by instinct until the mating season peaks in late September or early October.

The long legs of moose are ideally suited for wading through deep winter snow. Moose stretch their necks to pull down twigs and peel bark, leaving a browse line to mark the highest reach of their strong lips.

The antlers, sometimes as wide as a person is tall, will provide important calcium supplements to creatures who will gnaw on them once they have been dropped.

During winters with heavy snowfall, the forest floor, protected from winds that would disperse the snow in the high country, can be the scene of weakness and starvation. Unusually large snowfalls in 1989-90 caused many moose to starve or become sick from struggling through the deep snow. A thick ice crust on top of the snow can also be devastating to ungulates.

After most of the snow has melted and the moose start feeding on the earliest shoots of the year, pregnant cows give birth, usually to two calves. The calves stay with their mother for one year after which the cow chases them away. Frequently, only one of the two calves born to each cow will live through its first year. Bears and wolves love to eat moose calves for their first big meal of the spring, but a cow moose will fight heroically to defend her calves against them. She is a formidable opponent, even more aggressive than a bull in rut. Often she succeeds in driving the predators away from her young.

Wolverine

One of the most elusive animals in the forest, wolverines are solitary carnivores and require vast areas, ranging up to 500 square miles. Although they are slightly larger than a cocker spaniel, wolverines occasionally take down small caribou or moose. The larger carnivores, bears and wolves, will back off from a ferocious wolverine defending its cache. Their staple foods are hare and carrion. Like their cousins the mink, wolverines are prized for their pelts. Experienced parka makers claim the fur does not allow frost to build up and is soft and warm, ideal for lining the hoods of parkas.

S. Steinacher ©

Lynx

Lynx, a wild cat native to Alaska, prowl the spruce forest, alpine tundra and shrub communities in search of snowshoe hare. Lynx and hare are bound to each other in the cyclic choreography of predator and prey. If the hare population swells, so does the lynx population one or two years later; when hares are less abundant, fewer lynx kittens are born. Lynx travel up to five miles a day and have home ranges greater than a hundred square miles. Resembling house cats with short tails, tufted ears and large feet, lynx are about twice as large as their domestic counterparts. Lynx are hunted and trapped throughout most of Alaska.

Shrubby Transitions

As if to extract a toll from foot travelers passing from tundra to forest, or from forest to lakeshore, the shrublands reduce hikers to thrashing and cursing. Devil's Club lurks beneath the sprawling branches, and hikers are apt to surprise a brown bear because neither human nor bear is able to see more than a few feet ahead. The dense thickets of alder, willow and birch may be best appreciated from afar where one can marvel at the diversity of birdlife, the prime habitat for small animals, and this stage in the succession of plants. The understory of the alder and willow thickets

Trees and Shrubs

Alder *(Alnus sp.)*
There are three species of alder in Katmai: American green, Sitka, and thin leaf alder. Alders are recognized by their smooth bark with horizontal lines and tiny "cones". The tall shrubs grow in thickets along river beds, often with willows. Alders are a pioneer species in disturbed areas.

Kenai paper birch *(Betula papyrifera var. kenaica)*
An integral component of the spruce-birch forest that is widespread throughout Katmai, Kenai paper birch is slightly smaller than paper birch and has a darker, brown to reddish bark. Its leaves are a rounded triangular shape, notched, and turn a brilliant yellow in the autumn. Kenai birch is found only in Alaska.

Balsam poplar *(Populus balsamifera)*
Balsam poplar grows with white spruce and birch in boreal forest, with willows and alder in river bottoms, and on gravel bars.

Willow *(Salix sp.)*
There are 16 species of willow in Katmai ranging from low creeping shrubs to medium-sized trees.

Sitka mountain ash *(Sorbus sitchensis)*
Sitka mountain ash is not common and grows primarily in coastal forests.

Greene mountain ash *(Sorbus scopulina)*
Both mountain ashes in Katmai form large shrubs and small trees that grow in openings and clearings in forests. They have alternate compound leaves; leaflets have teeth and form pairs, except at the end. Greene mountain ash typically has 11- to 15 leaflets, while Sitka mountain ash has 9 to 11 leaflets. Both species have a reddish bark and are fragrant. The Dena'ina Indians favor ash for steambath switches. Their whitish flower clusters are showy and fragrant in June and July. Shiny bright red fruit clusters are bitter but used medicinally as are the inner bark and leaves. Made into tea or used fresh, mountain ash is used as a remedy for sore throats, tonsillitis, and tuberculosis.

Low Shrubs

Bog rosemary *(Andromeda polifolia)*
This spreading, evergreen shrub grows one- to two-feet tall in bogs and wet sedge tundra. Leaves are long and pointed, rolled at edges, hairless, shiny green on top and whitish beneath. Five bell-shaped pink flowers hang at the ends of branches.

Dwarf arctic birch *(Betula nana L.)*
This common spreading shrub is found in a range of environments from alpine tundra to muskeg. Its rounded wavy-edged leaves are sticky, bright green, and about _ inch across. It forms dense thickets and is eaten by moose and caribou.

Leatherleaf *(Chamaedaphne calyculata)*
One of the earliest flowering plants in the interior of Alaska, leatherleaf has small white flowers and dark green, leathery, elliptical leaves. It is a common evergreen shrub in lowlands throughout Alaska and grows to about three feet tall.

Devil's Club *(Echinopanax horridum)*
Sharp spikes cover the stems and very large leaves of this sprawling plant that grows in openings and ravines, alder thickets, and flood plain forests. Its fragrant white flowers bloom in June and the brilliant red berries stand out in the fall. The spikes, if embedded in the skin, will cause festering.

Narrow-leaf Labrador tea *(Ledum decumbens)*
Narrow-leaf Labrador tea is an evergreen shrub one- to two- feet tall that is common in tundra, sphagnum bog and spruce forests. It has narrow, dark green leaves rolled under at the edges and yellow-orange fuzz on the bottom. Small, white, fragrant flowers bloom in June and early July. Tea made from the leaves is used medicinally for weak blood, colds, tuberculosis, and as a laxative.

Sweetgale *(Myrica gale L.)*
A common shrub of wet boggy areas, sweetgale has long narrow leaves with several coarse teeth on the rounded tips, slightly hairy on both sides, and dotted with waxy yellow glands. Fruits are sticky nutlets; flower spikes for the coming year form late in the summer.

Shrubby cinquefoil/Tundra rose *(Potentilla fruticosa)*
This common shrub with yellow flowers blooms from June through August in many environments.

Kamchatka rhododendron *(Rhododendron camtschaticum)*
A flower common on dry rocky tundra, Kamchatka rhododendron is a small evergreen shrub with obovate hairy leaves and purple to deep red flowers.

Prickly wild rose *(Rosa acicularis)*
Pink flowers bloom in June and July; rosehips turn red in August, contain high levels of vitamin C, and are used in teas and jellies.

Beauverd spirea *(Spiraea beauverdiana)*
Beauverd spirea grows to two feet and is common in wet areas from lowland to tundra. Leaves are elliptic to ovate, up to two inches long, with teeth near the ends.

Berries

Bearberry/kinnikinnik
Arctostaphylos uva-ursi
Alpine bearberry (Ptarmigan berry) *Arctostaphylos alpina*
Pacific serviceberry
Amelanchier florida
Swamp gooseberry/Bristly black currant *Ribes lacustre*
Northern black currant
Ribes hudsonianum
Skunk currant
Ribes glandulosum
Northern red currant
Ribes triste
Nagoonberry
Rubus arcticus

Cloudberry
Rubus chamaemorus
Salmonberry
Rubus spectabilis
Pacific red elder
Sambucus callicarpa
Lowbush cranberry
Vaccinium vitis-idaea
Bog cranberry
Vaccinium oxycoccos
Early blueberry
Vaccinium ovalifolium
Bog blueberry
Vaccinium uliginosum
Highbush cranberry
Viburnum edule

might include low shrubs, herbs, grasses, ferns, and mosses.

Soggy Turf

Moist tundra is the legacy of the Ice Age. Like soggy carpet after a flood, the water-logged turf never managed to drain. It allows less water to seep out than precipitation supplies. Soil thickness can be nearly equivalent to soil moisture in this flat land. The water table is nearly horizontal, an inch of elevation can mean the difference between continuous and intermittent submersion in water. Continuously submerged soils are

Plants are gradually coloniz-ing the ashflow in the Valley of Ten Thousand Smokes.
JAMES GAVIN

deprived of oxygen, resulting in anaerobic conditions not suitable for many plants that need air. Sphagnum moss, spongy and saturated, seems to monopolize these areas. Insectivorous sundew plants consume a variety of insects for nitrogen since its not readily available in the highly acidic environment of the bogs. Organic acids turn the water brown and wild iris and cottongrass sprout from the mat.

Soils a fraction of an inch higher are only occasionally submerged and provide more optimal rooting conditions for most grasses and sedges. Shrubs that require a steady supply of soil gas tend to grow where they are rarely inundated. Here you find low shrubs such as crowberry, Labrador tea, low bush cran-

berry, dwarf birch, and arctic willow. Lousewort, monkshood, bistort and buttercup stand bright on the water-flecked tundra. Ducks, geese and other waterfowl make their homes in the ponds and grasses of the moist tundra.

Deep Bays, Clear Water

Clear cold waters ... deep bays surrounded by snow-topped peaks ... wild trout fighting on a dry fly — these are the images that, for many, mean Katmai. Five species of salmon swarm their way up the waterways from Bristol Bay, the richest salmon ground in the world, to the feeder creeks where they were born. The extraordinary network of lakes and rivers in Katmai comprises the greatest surface area of freshwater lakes in the national park system. Naknek, Grosvenor, Brooks, Kulik, Savonoski, Alagnak: the names alone stir one's soul. Born from the melting glaciers, the lakes and rivers are living watery communities.

Mergansers, loons, swans, flocks of ducks and other water birds live off the rich supply of foods furnished by these pristine lakes. Trout, grayling, Arctic char and salmon swim through the crystalline depths and turbulent streams. Beavers build lodges and dams on the rivers and ponds, floating logs on canals they have excavated. Playful river otters slide down rocks and twirl in offshore waters. The glaciers gave birth to the lakes; the lakes, beginning with the tiniest one-celled organisms, support the whole web of life in Katmai.

Common Fish of Katmai

The salmonids, a broad family of fish that includes salmon, trout, char, and grayling, are a primitive fish that evolved some 40 to 60 million years ago in the cold waters of the arctic. The original salmonid population spread world-wide, adapting in response to the diversity of conditions it encountered. Isolation and time worked their magic, leading to the evolution of the many species and subspecies of this family that exist today. Of the salmonids, five species of Pacific salmon, rainbow trout (a relative of the Atlantic salmon), grayling and char inhabit the waters of Katmai. Trout, salmon and char are part of one subfamily, *Salmonidae*, while grayling are classified as a different subfamily, *Thymallinae*.

SALMON

Although all five species of Pacific salmon find their way into the Brooks River, sockeye salmon are by far the most abundant. The five salmon species share similar life histories: hatching in the cold gravel riverbeds, they emerge as fry into the river, migrate to the sea, and return to spawn in the stream where they were born. Most people prefer sockeye and coho for eating.

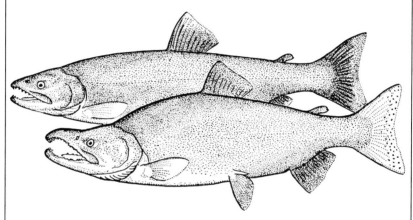

Sockeye (red) salmon *(Oncorhynchus nerka)*
Weighing six to 12 pounds, sockeye are medium-sized salmon. They have the most complex life cycle of all the salmon and travel the farthest inland to spawn. Sockeyes are identified by a lack of spots on the back and tail, and by the 30 to 40 long, fine, serrated, closely spaced gill rakers on the first arch. The sockeye run in Katmai peaks from late June through mid-July.

Coho (silver) salmon *(Oncorhynus kisutch)*
A popular game fish known for its strength and speed, coho reach 10- to 12 pounds and spawn in coastal rather than inland streams. Cohos are distinguished by small black spots on the back and on the upper lobe of the caudal fin. The coho run on the Brooks River is small and usually begins in late August.

All illustrations from *Freshwater Fishes of Northwestern Canada*, by J. D. McPhail and C. C. Lindsey. Bulletin 173, Fisheries Resource Board of Canada, Department of Fisheries and Oceans. 1970. Used with permission.

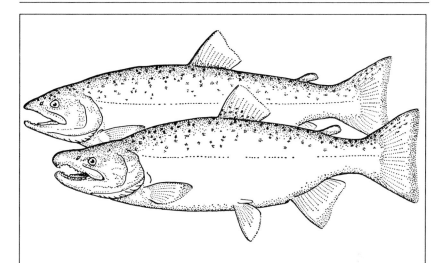

Chinook (king) salmon *(Oncorhynus tshawytscha)*

Chinooks are the largest of salmon, averaging 30- to 40 pounds and
sometimes exceeding one hundred pounds. They are a favorite trophy
salmon. Identified by small black spots on their back and tail, black lips,
and their large size, chinook are found in the Brooks and other rivers in
Katmai but generally prefer to spawn in larger rivers such as the
Columbia, Kenai and Yukon Rivers.

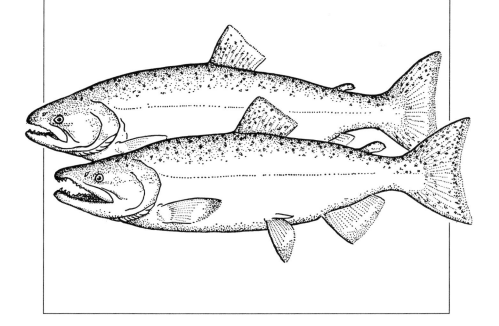

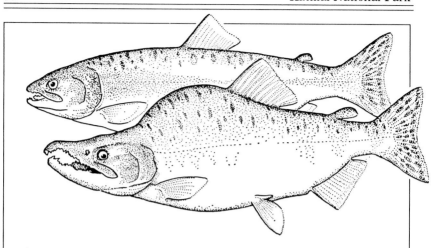

Pink (humpy) salmon *(Oncorhynus gorbuscha)*

At four to 10 pounds, pink salmon are the smallest of the Pacific salmon and are distinguished by large black spots on the back and on both lobes of the caudal or tail fin. They have the simplest life cycle and spawn in their second year. Their name refers to the body transformation the humpies experience upon reentering freshwater. Pinks are not common in Katmai.

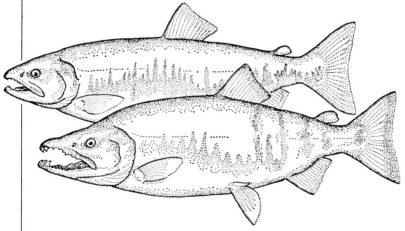

Chum (dog) salmon *(Oncorhynus keta)*

Similar to pinks, chums head for the sea almost as soon as they emerge as fry. They return to spawn in the fall of their third or fourth year, rarely traveling far inland. Averaging 10- to 13 pounds, chums lack distinct black spots on the back and tail, and have 18 to 28 short, stout, smooth gill rakers on the first arch. They are not abundant in Katmai.

TROUT & CHAR

Salmonids of the genus *Salvelinus* are known as char, but many are also commonly called trout (lake trout, for example). Rainbow trout and other fish of the genus *Salmo* are related to the Atlantic salmon.

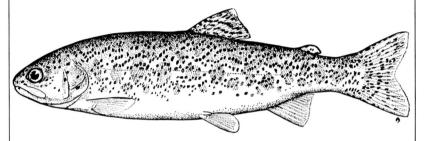

Rainbow trout *(Salmo gairdneri* Richardson*)*

Katmai boasts world-class wild rainbow trout; indeed, many visitors come equipped with a stack of rods and hundreds of flies that they employ in their search for a beautiful, fighting, trophy-sized rainbow. Aptly named, rainbow trout are blue-green- to-olive-colored on top, with flashy pink stripes down the sides, fading through silver into a pure white belly. Rainbows in Naknek and Iliamna Lakes may appear more silvery, resembling steelhead trout (rainbows that spend part of their lives in the ocean, but are not found in Katmai).

Rainbow trout are spring spawners, and a rainbow typically spawns for three to five seasons. The survival of the eggs is directly dependent on the amount of oxygen dissolved in the water, not only in the stream, but also in the gravel of the streambed where the eggs develop. Rainbow trout typically live up to five years but fish as old as nine years have been found. They usually weigh two- to four pounds but may achieve 10 pounds, and grow to lengths of six- to 24 inches or longer.

Lake trout *(Salvelinus namaycush)*

Alaska's largest freshwater fish, lake trout originally ranged throughout northern North America, extending as far south as the glaciers of the Ice Age. They prefer deep, cold lakes and stay as deep as possible during the summer. Lake trout eat whatever food is available: plankton, crustaceans, insects and clams.

They are identified by a dark green to grayish color, are covered with white or yellowish spots, and have a deeply forked tail. Like other char, lake trout spawn in the fall. Once they reach about age five, lake trout

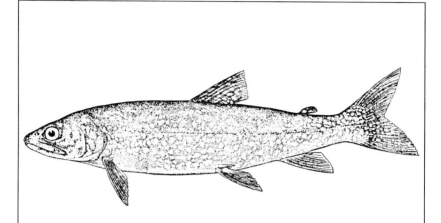

spawn every two- to three years, although farther south, they may spawn annually. During spawning season, males grow pale and develop dark stripes on their sides and around their heads. Lake trout live to be very old - the oldest recorded lake trout, taken in Chandler Lake, Alaska, was 42+ years old, weighed 27.5 pounds and was 37 inches long.

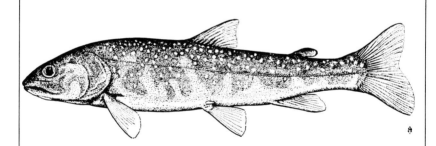

Dolly Varden *(Salvelinus malma)*

Dolly Varden are named after the woman in Charles Dickens's novel *Barnaby Rudge* who loved brightly colored dresses. They mature early, live for up to 20 years, not spawning until they are seven to nine years old, and stay fairly small, rarely exceeding six or seven pounds in Alaska.

This species is often confused with the Arctic char and the bull trout, and is best distinguished by pink or red spots that are smaller than the pupil of an eye. A small variety of Dolly Varden, the golden fin trout, lives in Idavain Lake. Stranded there as dropping water levels formed the waterfalls in Idavain Creek, the golden fin trout evolved independent of the rest of the population during the past 6,000 to 10,000 years.

Arctic Char *(Salvelinus alpinus)*

Arctic char have the northernmost range of all of the salmonids. It is difficult to distinguish them from Dolly Varden; the most diagnostic markings are pink- to red spots on their sides and back, the largest of which are bigger than the pupil of the eye. Arctic char spawn in the fall and typically weigh two- to 10 pounds although char weighing nearly 30 pounds have been caught in Canada. They feed heavily on sockeye fry in the Bristol Bay watersheds.

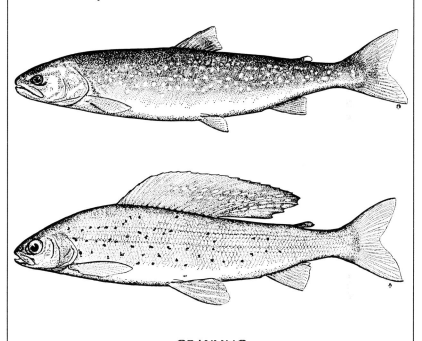

GRAYLING

Arctic grayling *(Thymallus arcticus)*

Identified by a gigantic dorsal fin and a tiny mouth, Arctic grayling do not attain large sizes, typically weighing only slightly more than one pound. Common throughout Alaska, grayling prefer pools in clearwater streams and lakes, winter in deeper pools, and spawn in gravels in early summer.

OTHER FISH

Other fish found in the fresh water of Katmai include: northern pike, burbot, whitefish, sticklebacks, slimy sculpin, and longnose sucker.

CHAPTER 5

The Earliest Inhabitants

Eskimos believe
Only bodies die
And the souls
Of the latest dead
Are inherited
By the newest born.

Ethel Davis [1]

The Aleutian Range—
A Natural Barrier

The steaming, snow-covered volcanos of the Aleutian Range must have appeared formidable to the villagers who lived on opposite sides of them, rarely crossing over. Societies flourished on both sides of the mountains for thousands of years, independent of those on the other side.

The past people of Katmai left houses, tools, and artwork that archaeologists have discovered and studied. The relics date from 3000 BC on the north side of the mountains and from 4000 BC on the Pacific coast of Katmai. The snowy volcanos on the skyline regularly spewed ash over the villages, leaving distinctive marker beds in the soil. These identifiable ash layers have helped archaeologists date the objects they find and piece together the history of these cultures.

---

(1) From *Silent Footfalls...A Poetic Adaptation of Alaska Native Legends.* Reprinted with permission of Ethel Davis and Blue Heron Press.

According to the archaeo-
logical evidence, the earliest
trade between people of the
Brooks River region and the
Katmai coastal people began
around 300 BC. By AD 1000,
cultural interaction was more
frequent as the people
swapped goods across Katmai
Pass.

Lives of the Eskimo

Salmon drove the lives of
the Brooks River-Naknek area
people. Using fish traps and
spruce root gill nets to capture
the fish, they put up enough
salmon to last through the winter, gutting it and hanging it
on racks to dry. The people
treasured raw salmon heads
during this season; these were
considered a special delicacy
when slightly putrefied.

In the village, two to four
families shared an under-
ground home, or *barabara,*
with a hearth in the central
common room. When the fish
supply was especially plentiful, they piled dried fish on the
floor as well as against the
inside walls, literally living
on top of it until the stockpile
was eaten down to expose the
floor.

The men of the village had
a *qasgiq*, or community house,
where ceremonies and festi-
vals marked the passing of the
seasons and filled the long
dark nights of winter with
laughter and joy. The entire
village would gather there to
dance to pounding drums, sing
songs of the past, feast on seal
oil and berries, and play stick
games and gamble. Dancers
wore elaborate masks repre-
senting the spirits of animals.

Eskimos throughout
Alaska believed that, after
death, people's spirits passed
into the bodies of animals.
They saw the spirits of their
ancestors in the animals and
respected the animals as family. Eskimos dressed in their
finest clothing when they
hunted sea mammals, wear-
ing exquisite ritual hunting

Man and woman from Kodiak Island, 1802.
BANCROFT LIBRARY, UNIVERSITY OF CALIFORNIA-BERKELEY

the Brooks River people would cross the Aleutian Range to hunt sea otter and other mammals and to gather shellfish.

The brown bear hunt was a test of endurance and courage, undoubtedly a profound experience for the lone hunter who attempted it. The hunter would respectfully address the bear as he approached, acknowledging its spirit. Then he threw a stick at the bear, inciting it to charge him and his weapon, a 20-foot long spear fitted with a blade a foot-and-a-half long.

As the bear impaled itself on the shaft, the hunter gripped the spear with all his strength, indeed his life depended on his grasp, and hoped the crosspiece would do its job to stop the bear. Connected by the wooden shaft, man and bear wrestled. The bloody and bruised hunter twisted the blade within the bear until, finally, it gave itself to the hunter and dropped onto the ground. After transporting the bear back to the village, often by boat, the hunter and his relatives would butcher and prepare the bear for its many uses. Brown bear skins were

hats to show their gratitude toward the animals who gave them their lives. Long bentwood hats or visors were molded using steam and decorated with intricate paintings, feathers, beaks, whiskers, and small carved charms. Ceremonial hunting hats have been found in the Bering Sea region dating back 2,000 years. One hat found in Katmai has ivory wings and drawings of a horned seal and a fish monster.

In the fall, the Brooks River people hunted caribou, bears and ptarmigan. They trapped and snared fox, marten, beaver and lynx. Wild berries, abundant in Katmai, were gathered and dried. Each year,

highly prized as door coverings.

Eskimos were expert kayakers, and baidarkas (kayaks) were the primary vessel for sea travel. They hunted whale, seal, sea lion and sea otter from baidarkas, using spears tipped with slate points poisoned with monkshood. Umiaks, larger sealskin boats resembling a skiff, were reserved for long journeys or wars. The spruce wood baidarka frame was held together by strips of split whalebone, and the whole vessel was encased in stretched sea lion, walrus or seal skin.

Eskimos took pride in wearing beautiful, finely-constructed clothing. The basic garment was the shirt-style *konagen*, later named parka by the Russians. Over their decorated animal-skin parka, the men wore apron-like squares of sea mammal skins belted low around their waist. Women wore sealskin sashes. They preferred parkas made from ground squirrel pelts, caribou, sea otter, or bird skins with feathers still attached. On top of their *konagen*, Eskimos frequently wore sealgut *kamleikas*, full-length anoraks, elaborately decorated with feathers, hair, skin, and embroidery. Cormorant skin *kamleikas* were worn for

Aleuts in their baidarkas, 1802.
BANCROFT LIBRARY, UNIVERSITY OF CALIFORNIA-BERKELEY

special occasions. Most of the time, the coastal people went barefoot. Only on long, overland journeys in cold weather did they wear boots. To top off their attire, they wore woven grass hats, decorated with feathers, beaks and paintings. Once trading with Europeans began, glass beads from around the world were made into beautiful women's headdresses.

As you wander in the Brooks River area, stepping over the former homes of the people who lived here more than 200 years ago, may you hear their whispers in the spruce and feel their spirits in the animals whose paths you cross.

The People of the Brooks River Area

The first people who settled in the Brooks River area subsisted on caribou. Bits of caribou bone remain in their temporary camps built on the shores of Naknek Lake and the Brooks River, along with stone lamps, knives and knife blades. Recent Katmai Natives called the Brooks River *Kittewick*, a name now applied to this period.

The people of the **Kittewick Period** (3000 BC to 1900 BC) may have been influenced by Shelikof Strait and coastal cultures. Although they were primarily inland hunters, they used oil-burning lamps and ground slate tools characteristic of these other cultures. Some of the camps in the Brooks River area may have been built by people from the Pacific side of the mountains who occasionally traveled inland to hunt caribou.

About 1900 BC, groups of people migrated from northern to southern Alaska, perhaps driven by a cooling climate. They brought with them aspects of an advanced culture adapted to the harsh conditions of the Arctic. Nicknamed *Gomers* by archaeologists for the tiny delicate tools they crafted, these people built the first permanent homes in the Brooks River area, settling at Brooks Falls, which has remained a popular location ever since.

The **Gomer Period** (1900 BC to 1100 BC) was the time of the **Arctic Small Tool Tradition** of southern Alaska. These people harvested salmon and hunted caribou, food sources reliable enough to enable them to settle in one area. Their homes had fireplaces, sloping entryways, and sod roofs; one can imagine them sitting by the fire in the winter chipping fine chalcedony points, bi-pointed endblades and adzes. The archaeologists who first unearthed the minuscule tools were so delighted by them they assigned elfish attributes to the former Brooks River residents. They held the Gomers responsible for causing mischief around their camp, such as taking notebooks and filling boots with water.

For 800 years the culture remained virtually unchanged. Then, Gomer Period people moved downriver, abandoning the Brooks River area for 800 years. Later cultures adapted to life on the coast, mastering the art of sea mammal hunting. People returned to the Brooks River around 300 BC, the first fully coastal people to live in the area. They harvested food from sea and land, and occasionally crossed the Aleutian Range to hunt sea mammals in the ice-free waters of Shelikof Strait. In the interior, they adapted their coastal skills for freshwater fishing.

The people of the **Brooks River Period** (400 BC - AD 1000) burned sea mammal oil in formed stone lamps, decorated fiber-tempered pottery with square or diamond checks, and used polished slate ulus and knives. Many elements of their culture were related to the Norton Sound culture. Other aspects were derived from coastal societies and from the Gomer Period people. Archaeologists have

Native barabara and storehouse near Naknek River, 1901. BANCROFT LIBRARY, UNIVERSITY OF CALIFORNIA-BERKELEY

identified several phases within the Brooks River Period, a complex time of settlement in Katmai. People in the Brooks River area continued hunting caribou and occasionally sea mammals, and fished for salmon, as they do today.

People began building homes with sunken arctic entries, making gravel-tempered pottery, and crafting ground stone tools of polished slate, major innovations which mark the beginning of the **Naknek Period** (AD 1000-1900). These same inventions developed in Thule Culture of northern Alaska just prior to their adoption in Katmai. During this time, the different Eskimo groups in Alaska interacted extensively with each other.

Late in the Naknek Period, the **Aglegmiut**, Pacific Eskimos from the Kuskokwim area, began moving south, reaching the northern shores of Bristol Bay in the late 1700s. They moved across the bay to the Alaska Peninsula, either pushing the residents further onto the peninsula or assimilating them. Relations between the Aglegmiut and the resident Natives were not always friendly. The 19th century Aglegmiut expansion was confined to the Bristol Bay coast, however, and Savonoski, in central Katmai, retained its identity. Even today, locals recognize the former residents of Savonoski, which was abandoned following the 1912 eruption of Novarupta, as different from the contemporary residents of Naknek. The two groups speak different dialects of Alutiiq, a sub-dialect of Yup'ik.

People of the Outer Coast

Nearly 6,000 years ago, a group of people established camps on the Katmai Pacific coast, on both the mainland and nearby islands. They lived in round houses in semi-permanent villages. These sites represent a people that settled much of the coastal region, including Kodiak, the Alaska Peninsula, and the Aleutians. The people of the **Takli Alder Phase** (4000 - 3000 BC), like their descendants, the Aleuts, hunted seal, sea lion, sea otter, cormorants and other birds.

Around 2500 BC, inhabitants of the coast began replacing their chipped stone tools with ground slate ulus, knives, bayonet points and other tools, a development that marks the **Takli Birch Phase** (2500 - 800 BC). The adoption of ground slate tools had little influence on other aspects of community life. People continued hunting sea mammals and, while no land mammal bones have been found in their camps, they may have crossed the Aleutian Range to hunt caribou. Archaeologists speculate that these people built the seasonal caribou hunting camps of the Kittiwick Period found at Brooks River.

If these sea-mammal hunting people dwelt on the Katmai coast over the next thousand years, they left no record of their lives. Punctuating the end of this 1,000-year gap were rough Norton-type fiber-tempered pottery and rectangular log homes with large stone hearths. The people who lived in these homes were descendants of the earlier Takli Birch population. The **Takli Cottonwood Phase** (AD 200 - AD 500) marks the shift from small encampments to permanent villages, and the advent of trading across the Aleutian Range.

As trading across the Aleutian Range intensified, the coastal people began to adopt customs from the other side of the pass. People of the **Kukak Beach Phase** (AD 500 - 1000) built homes with cold traps

---

Archaeological Resources Protection Act

Do not disturb any archaeological sites or artifacts you may encounter in Katmai. Please report any finding to a park ranger as soon as possible. It is illegal to excavate, damage, or remove artifacts from federal land and, if the damage exceeds $500, it is a felony. For more information, call 1-800-478-2724.

---

and sloping entryways, and made tools from chipped chalcedony rather than the ground slate that had been popular for the previous one thousand years. By AD 1000, the cultures on both sides of the mountain range were nearly identical. Labeled the **Kukak Mound Phase** (AD 1000 - 1500) on the coastal side, this period saw the rise of gravel-tempered pottery and the polished slate industry. Eskimos traded extensively across the mountains and throughout Alaska during this period, continuing a lifestyle which they maintained until the Russians arrived in 1741.

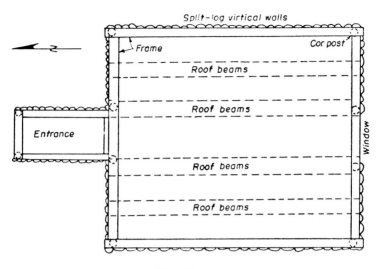

a. Plan View.

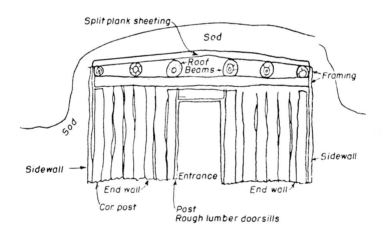

b. Side View of North Wall from Interior.

Semi-subterranean house structure, Savonoski.

From, W. A. Davis, *Archaeological Investigations*

Russian map of the Katmai coast, made about 1826.   LIBRARY OF CONGRESS

CHAPTER 6

The Europeans Arrive

The Russian Empire Discovers Alaska

The Russian empire of Peter the Great expanded like hot gas across Asia and Siberia during the early 1700s. Driven by the lucrative fur trade and the quest for new territory, the expansion was not to be halted by the Pacific Ocean. On his deathbed in 1725, the Russian ruler, Peter the Great, commissioned the Dane, Vitus Bering, to explore the fringes of his continent and North America. In 1728, Bering voyaged through the passage known today as Bering Strait. He returned to the continent on several more journeys and, in 1741, sailed to the Gulf of Alaska and established Russian sovereignty. The explorations ushered in a compelling but bloody period in Alaskan history.

The *promishlenniki*, the aggressive fur traders of the Kamchatka Peninsula, followed in Bering's wake. Inspired by the high volume of quality furs the Bering expedition had brought back, they began crafting crude vessels to sail to the Aleutians and southwest Alaska. Sergeant Emilian Bassoff, the first *promishlennik* to hunt eastward from Kamchatka, returned from his voyages with a half-million dollars worth of pelts. Russian traders, emboldened enough by their ignorance of the sea to brave the treacherous journey, traveled to Alaska in search of furs. The soft, waterproof coat of the sea otter was a treasured and profitable pelt, widely traded to the Chinese.

Although the *promishlenniki* were experienced at hunting sable, having driven the Asian animal to the brink of extinction, they lacked the knowledge to hunt the agile sea otter. To overcome this obstacle, some *promishlenniki* enslaved Aleuts, forcing parties of hundreds of men to spear otters from bidarkas while holding their wives and children hostage. By 1795, the *modus operandi* of many Russians was to conscript Aleuts, up to 1,400 at a time, for sea otter hunting expeditions. They forced the Aleuts to travel by bidarka as far as Sitka, 900 miles away in southeast Alaska, and commonly murdered Aleuts who refused to cooperate. Most of the Native hunters never returned to their villages. Swikshak Bay, Kaguyak, and Kukak Bay on the Katmai coast were inhabited when the Russians arrived.

At the same time, rampant hunting nearly wiped out the sea otter population. As competition intensified for the dwindling supply of pelts, the traders pushed east, arriving at Kodiak Island in 1763. The fiercely independent Koniag people were inhospitable and the Russians were discouraged from staying. Two Siberian merchants, Grigory Ivanovich Shelikhov and Ivan Golikov, returned to Kodiak in 1784.

Intent on dominating and controlling the entire North American fur trade, they founded the Shelikhov-Golikov Company post at Three Saints Bay on Kodiak Island. The rise of the Shelikhov-Golikov Company initiated a period of empire building in southwest Alaska as schools were constructed and Russian Orthodox missionaries arrived.

The company was wildly successful at entrenching its fur-trading monopoly. Shelikhov put together a consortium named the Russian American Company, to which the Czar of Russia granted exclusive dominion over Alaska in 1799. Alexandr Baranov, a company manager, moved its headquarters to Pavlovsk Harbor on Kodiak in 1793, where it remained the principal Russian outpost in Alaska until 1808, when the government and company headquarters moved to Sitka.

The Russian American Company extended its grasp across the Shelikof Strait to Katmai in 1799. It opened a trading post at Katmai village, which would remain an important village until the 1912 eruption of Novarupta.

The Russian rulers had shown little involvement in

Alaska during much of this time, leaving exploration and colonization to the traders. Catherine the Great was not pleased with the barbarous practices of the *promishlenniki* and adopted policies during her reign (1762-1796) which were intended to improve the treatment of Natives. Aleuts and some other Native groups were granted protection as imperial citizens, a standing equivalent to that of peasants in Russia.

The Russian Orthodox Church developed a strong presence in Native communities after the arrival of clergy in Alaska in 1794. With time, the Russian and Native cultures melded as the Natives adopted the Russian religion and language, and people from the two cultures intermarried.

After the Purchase

Shortly after the United States and Russia signed the treaty of transfer in April, 1867, a small party of Coast Guard scientists, headed by George Davidson, set sail to survey the natural resources of Alaska. In his report on the four-month voyage, Davidson recounted oil seeps, oil floating on lakes, and coal in Katmai and other areas of the Alaska Peninsula.

Another voyage in 1868 continued the studies, with Thomas Minor collecting natural history and cultural samples for the Smithsonian Institution. The United States Geological Survey sent the Becker-Dall expedition to conduct the first systematic survey of Alaskan minerals and resources in 1895, a program that continues today. The U.S.G.S. was not impressed with the mineral or petroleum resources of the Katmai area, and abandoned any thoughts it may have entertained about development.

After the United States purchased Alaska in 1867, the Alaska Commercial Company, an outgrowth of Hutchinson, Kohl & Co. of San Francisco, stepped into the shoes of the Russian American Company. The trading post at Katmai village changed hands along with many of the others.

With the change in trading partners, the price of pelts skyrocketed. The annual take of sea otter pelts tripled under American rule, as the Alaska Commercial Company encouraged the use of rifles to enhance production. Although sea otter hunting by non-Natives was illegal at the time, a man married to a Native woman was granted full Native rights with regard to hunting and trapping. This policy may have contributed to increased fur trading.

As the overhunted sea otter population dropped to near extinction in the late 1890s, trading slackened, and the Alaska Commercial Company pulled out of Katmai village.

The Natives, who had depended on fur trading to augment their livelihoods, suffered along with the slaughtered sea otters. As fur trading operations dwindled, salmon canneries moved in, as if to fill the void. Canneries sprang up in Kodiak, Cook Inlet, and the Aleutians in the 1880s, and two fish salteries were built at the mouth of the Naknek River. In Kukak Bay, on the outer coast of Katmai, a clam cannery was established, an oddity among the fish processing plants.

Fish processors soon showed their preference for European fishermen and Chinese laborers; in 1900, three canneries in Chignik employed 215 whites, 208 Chinese, and 12 Natives.

After the turn of the century, the fish processing plants began to hire more Natives. Residents of villages along the Katmai coast left their villages seasonally to work at the fish camps in Kodiak, Nushagak, Naknek, or elsewhere. Like sea otter hunting before them, the canneries would have a significant impact on the lives of the Native people in the Katmai area.

The Katmai Trail

Following a natural corridor from Katmai village on Shelikof Strait to Bristol Bay, the Katmai Trail has seen the feet of fur-trading Eskimos and wild-eyed prospectors. The U.S. Postal Service carried mail across the pass for a few years, and several heroic rescue teams struggled over the trail under fearsome winter conditions.

Shown on the first maps of the new territory produced by the U.S., the trail followed the steep Katmai River valley to Katmai Pass, the saddle between Mount Mageik, with its acidic pea-green crater lake and Trident Volcano, which erupted most recently in 1968. From the pass, the trail dropped to the floor of the valley known today as Valley of Ten Thousand Smokes, around Naknek Lake, and down the Naknek River to the village of Pawik near Bristol Bay. The route usually took at least four days to walk.

Most of the English-speaking wayfarers who traveled the Katmai Trail cursed the evil weather that resided on the dreaded Katmai Pass. The trail gained notoriety in articles written by Ivan Petroff, editor of *Alaska Appeal*, a journal supported by the Alaska Commercial Company. Petroff arrived in Alaska to conduct the U.S. Census and traversed the pass in 1880 during his survey explorations. A master of hyperbole, he furnished his readers with engaging descriptions of the journey. Petroff's party traveled with locals from Savonoski village. They received a magnificent reception upon their arrival at Katmai village.

Like other travelers expecting to find ship service at Katmai village, the party was disappointed, and had no choice but to cross Shelikof Strait with locals in bidarkas. Prior to attempting the crossing, the party consulted an astronome, an individual particularly attuned to the weather. The astronome failed to predict a turn in weather and Petroff's journey became an epic: 13 hours to Kodiak through thundering seas by moonlight.

The only known photo of Katmai Pass taken prior to the 1912 eruption.
From: J. E. Spurr, "A Reconnaissance in Southwestern Alaska in 1898," in U.S.G.S. 20th Annual Report.

B. SUMMIT OF KATMAI PASS.

A handful of other adventurers traversed the Katmai Trail on foot and by dogsled before the turn of the century. Many of these people hired Eskimo guides to accompany them. The route was well known to locals who had used it as a trade route for centuries. John Clark and writer Alfred Schanz, who earlier on their journey had made a detailed exploration of the Lake Iliamna-Lake Clark region, crossed the pass in February and March, 1891 by dogsled. Schanz was sent to Alaska by *Frank Leslie's Illustrated Newspaper* to obtain "exciting copy." The periodical printed his series "Our Alaska Expedition" throughout 1891. In these stories, Schanz identified, for the first time in print, the legendary saddle as Katmai Pass.

The Katmai Trail also was one of the final legs in George Fred Tilton's heroic dash from Barrow to San Francisco in the winter of 1897-98. Nine ships of an American whaling fleet were trapped in sea ice at Barrow that winter. The crew estimated the supplies would hold until July first, if strictly rationed. Unfortunately, a supply ship would not arrive by then, so the entire crew was in danger of starvation.

Ivan Petroff. From: R. A. Pierce, "New Light on Ivan Petroff," in *Pacific Northwest Quarterly*, vol. 59, no. 1.

Third mate George Tilton headed south with two Siberian natives and a dogsled team. The Siberians continued as far as Point Hope, where Tilton recruited an Eskimo couple, Tickey and Canuanar, to go with him. The trio continued south, obtaining supplies from missions and whaling camps, and killing at least two of their dogs for food. When they were three days short of St. Michael, they met two men from the revenue cutter *Bear* who had been enlisted by the whalers' families to drive a herd of reindeer to Point Barrow for the men. The reindeer drive seemed a dubious venture, so Tilton and the Eskimo couple continued toward the Yukon River, and from there to the Katmai Trail.

They reached Katmai village in March, 1898 to find four huts of Natives, no food, and one battered unseaworthy dory. They patched the dory with the last of Tilton's underwear and rowed the 37 miles to Kodiak Island. Tilton caught a ship to Portland, where he wired the owners of one of the whaling ships of the situation. They rejected his requests, not believing that he could have completed the 1,500-mile overland journey in the winter. Tilton finally convinced a ship owner to send supplies to the whalers. By the time it reached Barrow, the reindeer herd had arrived and the *Bear* had rescued those crew members who were sick. The supplies procured as a result of Tilton's run were used that summer by six whaling vessels that remained in the fleet.

Shortly after Tilton's heroic trek, prospectors discovered gold in Nome and soon stories flowed south like cheap whiskey. By 1899, gold fever was epidemic and the trickle of prospectors heading toward the Seward Peninsula grew to a flood. By August, 1899, more than fifty wooden buildings and hundreds of tents graced the beaches at Nome.

Unable to wait for summer to make the journey down the Yukon, would-be tycoons looked for overland routes. They used the Katmai Trail as a shortcut across the Alaska Peninsula, rather than sailing through the treacherous waters of the Aleutian Islands. The lone European trader at Katmai village built a bunk house to capitalize on the impatience of travelers. Hundreds of men crossed the pass en-route to Nome, whose population exploded to 25,000 as four million dollars in gold was extracted each year between 1900 and 1905.

During this period, the postal service also carried mail over the pass, although it only used this route for a few years. As the Nome Gold Rush ended, so too did much of the traffic on the Katmai Trail. The people of the Naknek area traded across the Katmai Trail through Katmai village, as they had for centuries, a practice which continued until the 1912 eruption of Novarupta forced the residents to evacuate.

Roy Fure's Cabin on the Bay of Islands

On August 30, 1912, 27-year-old Lithuanian immigrant Roy Fure (pronounced fury) landed in Sandpoint, Alaska aboard the *Ivanoff* from Vladivostok, Siberia. An immigrant who trapped and fished in rural Alaska, Fure originally visited Katmai in 1914. He spent that winter in the Naknek Lake vicinity. It was his first experience in the land where he would live for more than 40 years.

Fure built a log cabin on Naknek Lake's Bay of Islands in approximately 1926. He lived there with his wife Anna Johnson and their two children. He met Anna, a Native woman from Bethel, while working for Alaska Packers Association in Ugashik. Fure built the cabin of hand-hewn logs fitted together with finely crafted double dovetail joints.

In 1929, Anna Johnson died and Fure married Fanny Olson, an Aleut woman from Naknek. Their daughter, Nola Lillian, was born in 1930 at Kanatak near Becharof Lake. Nola grew up in the cabin at Bay of Islands. Fure had expanded the homestead through the years, displaying ingenuity and resourceful-ness. He built a windmill to generate power and fabricated sheds and an outhouse, lining them with flattened Blazo cans. He replaced the sod roof of the cabin with metal roofing, and built a trapline cabin on American Creek.

In 1931, Herbert Hoover extended the boundaries of Katmai National Monument. Fure and the other trappers who made their living within the new monument boundaries were ordered to leave. They appealed the order to Anthony J. Dimond, the Alaska Territory delegate to the U.S. House of Representatives. The National Park Service required that the trappers prove they were legitimate landholders under the settlement laws if they wanted to remain in the monument. In 1938, a special agent determined that Fure was not eligible to apply for a homestead because he was an alien. In 1941, Fure was arrested for trapping within the monument. He applied for U.S. citizenship in 1947, listing Fairbanks as his place of birth, and was granted citizenship.

About 1941, Fure built another cabin on American Creek. He continued to use both cabins until the time of his death. When he died in

Oregon in 1962, Fure willed his cabin and possessions to daughter Nola, who lived in Spenard, Alaska. She died in 1980, leaving no heirs. Trapper Jack, a Purple Heart Vietnam War veteran, began using Fure's cabin on American Creek in the 1970s. He lived and trapped there until at least 1978 when the government expanded the boundaries of Katmai and the cabins became the property of the National Park Service.

Roy Fure's log cabin still stands on the shore of Naknek Lake next to the trail from Bay of Islands to Grosvenor Lake. This trail was tramped into existence by the hardy trappers who settled in the Katmai area 75 years ago. The cabin, used today by canoers and kayakers paddling the Savonoski Loop, was added to the National Register of Historic Places in 1985. It was renovated by the National Park Service in 1986-88 to near original condition and is used as a ranger station during the summer.

Fure cabin after 1991 refurbishment.
JAMES GAVIN

Explosion in the Ring of Fire

The Katmai Mountain blew up with lots of fire, and fire came down trail from Katmai with lots of smoke. We go fast Savonoski. Everybody get in bidarka. Helluva job. We come Naknek one day, dark, no could see. Hot ash fall. Work like hell.

American Pete
Chief of Savonoski
1912 [1]

"A mountain has burst..."

Forewarned by the jolting and rumbling of the earth for several days before the colossal eruption, many of the Natives fled their villages, collecting drinking water in preparation for what they expected would be a large blast. Indeed, the explosion that shook Katmai on June 6, 1912 was the most voluminous volcanic eruption of the twentieth century, the largest eruption of its kind in 1,800 years. In spite of the monstrous size of the violent outburst, few people witnessed it and, miraculously, nobody was killed or hurt.

American Pete and his party were the only people in the Ukak Valley at the time of the eruption. On the other side of the range, the entire population of Katmai village was away fishing during the eruption except two families who remained in the village until June 4. Shaken by the nearly continuous earthquakes that rocked the area with increasing intensity, they climbed into a dory and rowed toward Cold Bay.

[1] Quotes from Robert Griggs and other National Geographic authors as indicated in text chapter are reprinted with permission from the National Geographic Society and *National Geographic Magazine*.

C.L. Boudry of Cold Bay interviewed the two families after their arrival, and wrote in his journal:

Two families arrived from Katmai scared and hungry and reported the volcanoes up 15 mile from Katmai [village] to the left of Toscar trail and that one-half the hill blun up and covered up everything as far as they could see also that small rock were falling for 3 or 4 miles at sea but could not say more of it as every *thing es closed up with smoke. These people had left Katmai village June 4 and camped between Kashvik and Alinchak bays. The rocks an fall in their boat are of the size of coarse rice and of the pumice stone formation. No one es lost as far as they know but all the natives are east of Katmai and the main flow of smoke go there as a strong SW wind blowing so they are in a bad shape.*

They report the Katmy hill blew up and threw rock out to sea, but could not tel mor as they whare on the road to Cold Bay — an that pommey stone in fire whas falling 20 miles an that the watter was hot in the Katmy bay — after examining ther boat ther i found pummice stone the sise of common rice.

Ashfall buries a house in Kodiak, more than 60 miles from Mount Katmai. ANCHORAGE MUSEUM OF HISTORY AND FINE ART

Jack Lee of Cold Bay wrote in his diary:

They report the top of Katma Mountain blun of. There was a lot of Pummy stone in their dory when they got here and they say Hot Rock was flying all eraund them.

Kaflia Bay, 30 miles from the crater, was sheltered from the heavy ashfall by the mountains that also blocked the view of the volcano.

The Terrible Blackness

The First Blast

Left Uyak at 8.45 a.m., June 6; strong westerly breeze and fine clear weather. At 1 o'clock p.m., while entering Kupreanof Straits, sighted a heavy cloud of smoke directly astern, raising from the Alaska Peninsula. I took bearings of same, which I made out to be Katmai Volcano, distance about 55 miles away. The smoke arose and spread in the sky, following the vessel, and by 3 p.m. was directly over us, having traveled at the rate of 20 miles per hour.

*Kaflia Bay
June 9, 1912*

My dear Wife Tania:

First of all I will let you know of our unlucky voyage. I do not know whether we shall be either alive or well. We are awaiting death at any moment. Of course do not be alarmed. A mountain has burst near here, so that we are covered with ashes, in some places 10 feet and 6 feet deep. All this began on the 6th of June. Night and day we light lamps. We cannot see the daylight. In a word it is terrible, and we are expecting death at any moment, and we have no water. All the rivers are covered with ashes. Just ashes mixed with water. Here are darkness and hell, thunder and noise. I do not know whether it is day or night. Vanka will tell you all about it. So kissing and blessing you both, good-bye. Forgive me. Perhaps we shall see each other again. God is merciful. Pray for us.

*Your husband,
IVAN ORLOFF*

The earth is trembling; it lightens every minute. It is terrible. We are praying.

So wrote Capt. C.B. McMullen of the steamer *Dora*, which happened to be passing through Shelikof Strait at the time of the eruption. McMullen's observations give the first indication of the time of eruption, and also identified Mt. Katmai as being involved in the eruption. Sixty miles (100 kilometers) from the crater of Katmai, across Shelikof Strait in Kodiak, people saw the ash cloud rushing toward them. About 5 p.m. on Thursday, June 6, the sky suddenly darkened and heavy ash began to fall on Kodiak. By 6:30 that night, the thick ash blotted out all daylight. As the ash fall decreased during the night and stopped by mid-morning, the Kodiak Islanders breathed a sigh of relief, not knowing they would soon be submerged in an even thicker blackness that would last for two more days.

The Second and Third Eruption

Ashes began to fall again at noon on the 7th, choking the air, and producing a darkness so thick that the terrified inhabitants could not see the light from a lantern held at arms length.

J.E.Thwaites, mail clerk of the steamer *Dora*, which was passing by during the eruption, wrote in his log:

And now began the real rain of ashes; it fell in torrents; it swirled and eddied. Gravity seemed to have nothing to do with the course of its fall. The under side of the decks seemed to catch as much ash as the sides or the decks under our feet. Bright clusters of electric light could be seen but a few feet away, and we had to feel our way about the deck.

The officers of the deck had to close the windows of the pilothouse tightly, and even then it was with the greatest difficulty that the man at the wheel could see the compass, through the thick dust that filled the room.

In the meantime, lurid flashes of lightning glared continuously round the ship, while a constant boom of thunder, sometimes coinciding with the flash, increased the horror of the inferno raging about us. As far as seeing or hearing the water, or anything pertaining to earth, we might as well have been miles above the surface of the water. And still we knew the sun was more than two hours above the horizon.

In the saloon everything was white with a thick layer of dust, while a thick haze filled the air. The temperature rose rapidly, and the air, what there was left of it, became heavy, sultry, and stifling. Below deck conditions were unbearable, while on deck it was

worse still. Dust filled our nostrils, sifted down our backs, and smote the eye like a dash of acid. Birds floundered, crying wildly, through space, and fell helpless on the deck.

Evacuees from Kodiak on board the *Manning* anxiously await their fate, 1912.
© NATIONAL GEOGRAPHIC SOCIETY

When the third day dawned dark with ashfall, the people of Kodiak decided to evacuate the village. Hundreds of terrified souls piled on board the *Manning*, a U.S. Revenue Cutter that was coaling in Kodiak, and into the storehouse at the wharf. The ship stayed moored at the dock until afternoon, when the crew decided to make a break for the other side of the island during a lull in the ashfall, not knowing if they would get another opportunity to sail.

The people who had crowded onto the *Manning* could hear landslides booming down the slopes of Kodiak Island, but still could not see which mountain was erupting. During these days of dread, the *Manning* accommodated nearly 500 people, more than four times the number it was built for. By the time the ashfall finally dwindled out on the morning of June 9th, Kodiak had experienced two days and three nights of nearly unbroken darkness. The island was cloaked under gray drifts several feet high and porches and roofs lay crushed under mounds of the fine grit.

The sound of the explosion was heard throughout Alaska on the morning of June 6: in Juneau, 750 miles away; in Fairbanks, 500 miles northeast; and in Dawson, 650 miles northeast. Acid rain produced by the sulfurous clouds burned people's skin and eyes in Cordova, eating into metal roofs and killing all the vegetation in Seward on June 11. At Cape Spencer, 700 miles to the east, fumes tarnished brass within 20 minutes after it was polished. Two feet of ash covered an area of 2,500 square miles and dust fell in Puget Sound, 1,500 miles away, obscuring the sun and dissolving linen in Vancouver with its acidity.

The Exploding Earth

Geologists have pieced together the story behind these amazing events.

The eruption began with a violent explosion that took half of Falling Mountain with it as a geyser of molten rock burst into the atmosphere, propelled 25 miles (30-40 kilometers) into the air. The initial blast ripped a hole through the sedimentary rocks as if they were paper. Following the first blast, pulses of magma spewed from the earth.

The gases that had been held in the magma by the super-pressurized conditions within the earth fizzed from the molten rock as it spouted from Novarupta like a can of soda shaken up and opened. These gases more than doubled the volume of the frothy magma as it spilled from the vent. As if gushing from an exploding pressure cooker, the vaporized rock quickly cooled into a chaos of airborne ash, pumice, and glassy rock.

It flooded out at a tremendous rate, gliding on a layer of air as it rushed down the valley. As if on a water slide, the steamy mixture of pumice, ash, and magma, known to geologists as a *nuée ardente*, zoomed down the valley with practically no friction to slow it. It sloshed up the sides of the Ukak valley leaving high ash marks on the Buttress Range 90-180 feet (30-60 meters) above the current valley floor. As the ash flow slowed, it settled down, releasing gases and cooling. Subject to the pressure of the overlying rock and its own internal heat, the unit solidified into welded tuff.

By the time the ash flow had traveled 10 miles (16 kilometers) down the Ukak valley, it had lost its momentum, no longer possessing the force to flow over the glacial moraine near today's Three Forks Overlook. A few fingers of the ash flow managed to spill over low areas in the moraine, and continued another three miles (five kilometers) down-valley engulfing but not toppling trees. These barkless trees stand today as a "ghost forest," in contrast to the charred wood eroded from the ash that can be found along the Ukak River below the Three Forks Overlook.

As the magma erupted from the earth, it emptied great interconnected magma chambers beneath Mount Katmai and Novarupta. Mount Katmai, which had dominated the skyline at 7500 feet before the eruption, collapsed under its own weight as the magma supporting it was ejected. Because it collapsed, everyone mistakenly believed that Mount Katmai was the vent of the eruption. Not until 1953, when Garniss Curtis showed that the ash thickened systematically toward Novarupta and not Mount Katmai, was Novarupta revealed as the true vent of the eruption.

Three volcanos in the Mount Katmai vicinity, Mount Katmai, Trident Volcano, and Novarupta, are linked by one underground plumbing system. The collapse of Mount Katmai during the 1912 eruption of Novarupta clearly shows the connection between those two centers, but Novarupta is actually closer to Trident. In fact, if it weren't for the collapse of Mount Katmai, Novarupta might be considered a flank vent on Trident. The fracture patterns around Novarupta indicate that the magma was transported to it through dikes, possibly via a chamber beneath Trident. The prominent hill northeast of Novarupta dome is known as the Turtle. It was probably uplifted by a rising magma body that stopped before it penetrated the ground surface. The Turtle was fractured by the event, and grabens, or drop-block faults, are evident on the hill.

A mere pimple in the ranks of the large Aleutian volcanos of the Katmai group, Novarupta in all likelihood never erupted before 1912. More than half a mile (one kilometer) in diameter and in depth, the vent was backfilled with the ash it had released. The last bit of lava to ooze out

A Story of Banded Pumice and Magma Chambers

Swirled together like marble cake, the black-and-white-banded pumice thrown from Novarupta during the 1912 eruption tells a story of origins and explosions, of subterranean chambers churning with molten rock.

Silica, the most abundant mineral on earth, appears as an ingredient in most rocks that form the earth. Indeed, as flour is to baked goods, silica is one of the most basic ingredients of rocks and minerals. It is the only mineral in quartz, opal and chert, as well as in common window glass. It is a major component in magma and in the igneous and volcanic rocks formed from the magma.

The amount of silica in a magma determines how it behaves and looks when it reaches the surface. Magma containing a lot of silica (70 percent) is viscous like honey, and is described as rhyolitic. Magma with less silica (50 percent) is thinner, more like water, and is called basaltic. Magmas with silica content intermediate between these two cool to form andesite and dacite.

Even today, gobs of hot magma stream upward through the earth's crust from the subduction zone beneath Katmai. Driven by differences in density and temperature, irresistible to the equalizing laws of nature, probably hundreds of magma bodies surge toward the surface. Many of the plumes bore right through the earth into the atmosphere, erupting as the volcanos of the Aleutian chain.

The composition of the magma when it reaches the surface affects how it erupts. If it is rhyolitic, the high silica content resists the release of volatile gases and forces the pressure to build in the magma chamber. When the pressure is great enough to break through the surface, the result is often an explosive eruption. In contrast, basaltic magma tends to seep out, spilling like water from an overfilled bucket. The Hawaiian volcanos are basaltic in composition. Mt. St. Helens is primarily andesite and dacite.

The first eruptive blast from Novarupta in 1912, the geyser of magma that shot 25 miles into the air, was almost pure high-silica rhyolite. Highly unusual for the Aleutians — only one other occurrence of such high-silica rhyolite is known there — the rhyolitic eruption of Novarupta was short-lived.

After the initial blast, the rest of the eruption was dacitic and andesitic in character. Dacitic materials spewed from the vent after the rhyolite, followed by andesitic magma and ash. Where the white rhyolite and the black andesite and dacite cooled together, they formed banded pumice. Observed for one of the first times in the Valley of Ten Thousand Smokes, banded pumice such as this alludes to the intermixing of these three types of magma.

MODERN GLACIERS OF KATMAI

The glaciers in Katmai today are remnants of the massive glaciers of the Ice Age that reached all the way from the tops of the volcanos to Bristol Bay. Five glaciers, known as the Knife Creek Glaciers, had their origin atop Mount Katmai. Cut off from their source when the mountain collapsed in 1912, the glaciers lie stagnant, blanketed with ash. Since 1912, the snows that maintained the Knife Creek Glaciers continued to fall, building up new glaciers inside the caldera of Mt. Katmai. These may be the only glaciers in the world whose exact age is known.

Father Hubbard's expeditions took precautions against the unknown dangers.
HUBBARD COLLECTION, SANTA CLARA UNIVERSITY ARCHIVES

of the vent solidified to form the lava plug known as Novarupta dome. By the time Novarupta sputtered to the end of its 60-hour outburst, 4.8 cubic miles (20 cubic kilometers) (dense rock equivalent) of air-fall tephra and up to 3.6 cubic miles (15 cubic kilometers) of ash-flow tuff had blanketed the surrounding lands.

Expeditions to the Volcanic Land

Josiah Edward Spurr, leader of the 1898 U.S. Geological Survey expedition that visited Katmai, wrote the only known geological observations of the Valley of Ten Thousand Smokes prior to the 1912 eruption. Spurr's report was of primary interest to Robert Griggs as he searched for accounts of the valley before the eruption. Spurr described Katmai Pass as lying between two extinct volcanos, but said that the Natives reported that one of the volcanos occasionally smoked. Griggs was not able to determine which of the volcanos they referred to.

Reported Spurr, "Extensive hot springs emerge from the Katmai side of the mountains below the pass, and there are very frequent earthquakes and other evidences of volcanic activity. Our party itself experienced a slight earthquake just after crossing." These observations foreshadowed the explosive eruption that would rock Katmai 14 years later.

As soon as the eruption began, George C. Martin of the U.S. Geological Survey began organizing an expedition in conjunction with the National Geographic Society. The expedition arrived by ship in Kodiak just four weeks after the eruption began. The party landed in Katmai village but did not travel inland or study the volcano. Rather, Martin spent his time interviewing the people who had witnessed the eruption, obtaining written reports of observers, and sampling and measuring the thickness of ash on Kodiak.

In 1913, botanist Robert F. Griggs of the National Geographic Society traveled to Kodiak to study revegetation of the ash deposits. He found the formerly green hills of Kodiak so barren and desolate that he doubted they would ever thrive again.

Griggs returned to Kodiak in 1915 to continue the revegetation study, with instructions from the National Geographic Society to make only a hasty reconnaissance of the volcanic district. He was shocked by the abundance and strength of the vegetation in Kodiak; it surpassed even the lush pre-eruption condition. The ash had enhanced plant growth, not by fertilizing the plants but, rather, by acting as a mulch. New plants sprang from the old root systems that had lain dormant in the soil for up to two or three years. Horsetails prospered as never before, growing through up to 36 inches of ash and sending runners into the ash from their central rootstocks. They acted as a binder and enabled other plants to gain a toehold in the shifting medium. Many plants could sprout only where the ash blanket fractured as it contracted, providing thin zones that the shoots could pierce.

After leaving Kodiak, the 1915 expedition members landed in Katmai village. They reached the lower slopes of the volcano but lacked the time

Mr. and Mrs. Robert Griggs at Baked Mountain.
© NATIONAL GEOGRAPHIC SOCIETY

to proceed further. Griggs left Katmai convinced that an extensive exploration of the valley and volcanic district was warranted, and set about organizing one for the following year.

In 1916, Robert F. Griggs led the fourth National Geographic expedition to the area. His experience during the previous year persuaded Griggs that a packer was needed to assist with the expedition. He approached the chief of Kodiak, who said, "Me no Katmai" and advised his neighbors that "Life better than money." In spite of these warnings, Griggs found a man, Walter Metrokin, the famous one-handed bear hunter of Kodiak, who was willing to go. The five men landed on the south side of Katmai valley and ascended Mount Katmai on July 19.

On July 31, they crossed the Katmai Pass and saw, for the first time, the Valley of Ten Thousand Smokes. When Griggs and his companions laid eyes on the valley, they were enchanted and disturbed by the sight of the gargantuan columns of steam that rose to the sky through the newly emplaced ash flow. Some of the smokes appeared as marble pillars, others as walls,

rising pure white from holes and fissures in the ash. Griggs described the vision they saw before them:

As far as one could see down the broad flat-floored valley, great columns of white vapor were pouring out of the fissured ground and rising gracefully, until they mingled in a common cloud which hung between the mountain walls on either side. We could not see how far the activity extended, for about five miles down the valley the smoke had entirely closed in, cutting off any further view in that direction.

Dazzled by his fleeting glimpse of the rising columns of steam, Griggs resolved to return for a full exploration of the district the following year.

The mandate of the 1917 expedition was to explore the Valley of Ten Thousand Smokes. Griggs took six months making arrangements, preparing food, and selecting hardy members for the expedition. He decided the 10 expedition members had no choice but to carry supplies themselves up the Katmai River and over the pass to the Valley of Ten Thousand Smokes.

The experience of the party members was nearly overwhelming. Griggs wrote, "For

NATIONAL GEOGRAPHIC SOCIETY

"Just in front was our cook-stove — a mild-mannered fumarole — into which we hung our pots to cook our food. We were somewhat dubious beforehand as to the feasibility of this method of cooking because of the noxious gasses that came off along with the steam, but the results were more than satisfactory…

Since the pots were surrounded by an atmosphere of live steam just at the point of condensing, nothing ever boiled away, cooked to pieces, or burned, no matter how long neglected or forgotten.

There was only one drawback: while we were in the valley we had to do without our old standbys, bacon and flapjacks, for our stove would not fry. There were, however, many vents in the valley quite hot enough to fry bacon."

Robert Griggs

"Directly opposite the precipices of Falling Mountain lies Novarupta, the greatest of all the vents in the valley. This, though newly formed at the time of the big eruption, is one of the world's largest volcanoes… it burst through in a new place along the margin of the old volcanic complex, appearing not in igneous rock, but in sedimentary sandstone adjacent to former igneous extrusions."

Robert Griggs

the first few days we were over-awed. For a while we simply could not think or act in the ordinary way. At night I would curse myself, as I lay in my blankets, and make a list of the things I wanted to do the next day; but when the morning came I could not move myself to action. I could only look and gape."

The expedition members were terrified of falling through the fragile crust. They discussed whether to rope up while crossing the crust and decided it would be more humane not to, letting a man who should break through flounder to his demise in a pit of hot acid rather than pull him scalded from beneath the crust.

The emotions these men felt upon walking into the

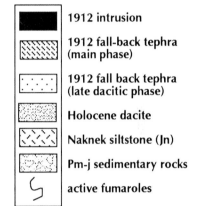

LEGEND

1912 intrusion

1912 fall-back tephra (main phase)

1912 fall back tephra (late dacitic phase)

Holocene dacite

Naknek siltstone (Jn)

Pm-j sedimentary rocks

active fumaroles

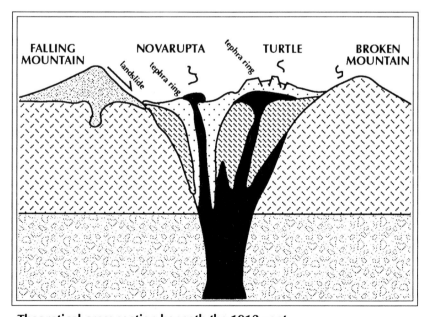

Theoretical cross section beneath the 1912 vent.
JOHN EICHELBERGER, GEOPHYSICAL INSTITUTE, UNIVERSITY OF ALASKA-FAIRBANKS, 1991

"For the first few days we were overawed. For a while we simply could not think or act in the ordinary way. At night I would curse myself, as I lay in my blankets, and make a list of the things I wanted to do the next day; but when the morning came I could not move myself to action. I could only look and gape."

Robert Griggs

Valley of Ten Thousand Smokes are hinted at by a few of the names they bestowed on the land. The River Lethe, which was nearly dry because its turbid water vaporized instantaneously when it crossed the hot ashflow, was named for the river that, in Greek mythology, flowed through the center of hell. Mount Cerberus crouches at the head of the Valley of Ten Thousand Smokes, an incarnation of the three-headed dog who guarded the gates of hell. During Griggs's time, Cerberus was nearly surrounded with fuma-

roles. Falling Mountain rumbled constantly as boulders and rockslides tumbled down its shattered flanks.

The fumaroles that gained the valley its name were formed as the ash flow deposits, 1400° to 2000°F (800° to 1000°C) when they erupted, contacted the streams, groundwater, and snow cover of the valley. The water and snow vaporized immediately into steam, forcing its way up through a profusion of channels to the surface of the ash deposit. The hot steam dissolved minerals from the ash, combining with fluorine, chlorine, carbon dioxide and sulfur to produce weak acids that enhanced the leaching.

When the steam contacted the cool rocks at the surface, the minerals precipitated as brilliantly colored encrustations. The colors that ring the fossil fumaroles, still visible today, are caused by mineral depositions: hematite (red), magnetite (black), pyrite (gold), sulfur (yellow), gypsum (white or clear), arsenic sulfide (orange), and iron sulfides (blue).

Griggs found mosses, algae, lichens, and liverworts growing in the steamy warmth of the fumaroles in the Valley of Ten Thousand Smokes.

Other small species moved in where these pioneer plants had stabilized a bit of soil.

Following the 1917 expedition, Griggs and other expedition members were anxious to return to the Valley of Ten Thousand Smokes to obtain scientific data. However, a major scientific expedition was postponed until 1919 because of World War I.

A small expedition was sent in 1918. It consisted of only two men, Sayres and Hagelbarger, who had been members of the 1917 expedition. Their mission was to study the fumaroles, or smokes, in part to predict their longevity.

This time the men did not approach the valley from Kodiak, as the previous expeditions had, but circled around the Alaska Peninsula to Bristol Bay and ascended up the Naknek River and Naknek Lake. They concluded from their investigation that the fumaroles would continue steaming. Their findings were instrumental in convincing the president to designate Katmai as a national monument later that year, but their prediction concerning the longevity of the smokes was proven false within 20 years.

In 1919, the National Geographic Society sent the largest expedition yet, nineteen scientists and assistants. This expedition approached from Bristol Bay, hauling supplies by power dory up the Naknek River and Naknek Lake. The first tourists also came to Katmai that year: one man from Portland, Oregon, and three women who were the wives of expedition scientists.

Dr. Robert F. Griggs devoted much of his career to exploring and studying the Valley of Ten Thousand Smokes. His *National Geographic* articles and photographs, and his 1922 book, *The Valley of Ten Thousand Smokes*, remain the definitive references on the history and explorations of the remarkable valley.

"I found my matter-of-fact chemist was counting the smokes to see whether I had been justified in asserting that there were ten thousand of them. He soon announced that I was quite well inside the number."

Robert Griggs

Another explorer who visited the Valley of Ten Thousand Smokes in the first decades after the eruption was Father Bernard Hubbard, an adventurous, amiable Jesuit priest. He traveled the wilds of Alaska for more than thirty years in the name of geology. Perhaps best known for his explorations of Aniakchak Crater, Hubbard visited Katmai and the Valley of Ten Thousand Smokes with his students from Santa Clara University in 1928, his second year traveling to Alaska. His stories of "the terrible grandeur of Katmai, the cradle of the storms, the dragon's nest" (Katmai caldera), and the Valley of Ten Thousand Smokes titillated readers of the *Saturday Evening Post* and *National Geographic* for many years.

A number of geological teams have traveled into the Valley of Ten Thousand Smokes over the years, including several in recent years whose ongoing research continues to unravel the story of the 1912 eruption.

Hubbard party camping amidst the devastation.
HUBBARD COLLECTION, SANTA CLARA UNIVERSITY ARCHIVES

The Dying of the Smokes

As the ash deposits cooled during the twenty years after the eruption, they were no longer hot enough to vaporize surface water. As a result, the fumaroles, or smokes, gradually stopped steaming. Eventually, nearly all of them stopped.

A few fumaroles still exist near Novarupta, Baked, Broken, and Falling Mountains where groundwater seeping through fractures encounters the still warm rock beneath Novarupta. These remaining fumaroles, in contrast to the short-lived "rootless" fumaroles that created the spectacular impression of the Valley of Ten Thousand Smokes, are in contact with a deep heat source. When the smokes died out, so did most of the plants that depended on the moisture and heat of the fumaroles.

Although the fumaroles no longer steam, the Valley of Ten Thousand Smokes seems today, as it did 75 years ago, to be too awesome to be a part of the rest of the world, not quite connecting up with the "little things which are built into our lives." An elemental emptiness hovers over the tan pumice slopes and the crusty ochre and rust fossils of Griggs's smokes. Lichen grows only in the wind shadow of pebbles embedded in the tephra. The River Lethe defies reason, churning with ferocity through three-dimensional space: here wide and raging, there a twisting snake of a river narrow enough to step across. People have died for taking too small a step. There is a purity to being in a land so free of human embellishments, so windy that thoughts are whisked from the mind like pebbles of pumice. I feel in the emptiness not desolation but freedom.

In the ashy highlands, cut through with new erosion, bear tracks cross the mineral pumice. No lichen grows here, certainly not grass, nor berries, nor other earthly plants. I wonder what brings brown bears to this country: were they only passing through, or do even bears wander through this land, listening to the wind whisper across the ash?

"Pictures cannot bring back the Valley of the Smokes…
They seem too big to be a part of the rest of the world.
They do not seem to connect up with the little things
which are built into our lives.

Outstanding in my memory is the valley as I left it. It
was a brilliant day, with puffy silver clouds that floated
on a sky of deepest blue and sunlight that glinted on
opalescent steam jets and sparkled on peaks fresh-
capped with snow.

As, homeward bound, we skirted Cerberus, the steamers turned in the dying sunlight to shimmering gold and the snowy crests of distant mountains glinted yellow. I forgot the heavy pack which bowed my shoulders as I glanced backward at the the growing beauty which filled the valley. Through its giant gateway, the Valley of Ten Thousand Smokes sank from sight as we dropped over the pass, and the sky above reddened to a crimson halo in the fading rays of the sinking sun."

D. B. Church
1917 National Geographic
Expedition Member

CHAPTER 8

The Preservation of Katmai

Katmai Monument serves no purpose and should be abolished.

Thomas Riggs Jr.
Alaska Territorial
Governor, 1920

Creating the Monument

Robert F. Griggs and the other expedition members returned from Alaska with the steaming fumaroles and glaciated volcanos of the Valley of Ten Thousand Smokes etched into their memories. Griggs's stories and pictures in *National Geographic* were read in countless wartime living rooms, helping inflame a generation with a spirit of adventure and lust for exploration. Griggs considered the Valley of Ten Thousand Smokes to be an outstanding, and possibly the greatest,

natural wonder of the world.

A youthful conservation movement swelled through the United States at that time, resulting in the formation of the National Park Service in 1916, even as Griggs struggled over the Katmai Pass. In the fervor of the preservation movement, it was only natural that the Valley of Ten Thousand Smokes should be set aside as a national monument.

Professor Griggs and his sponsor, Dr. Gilbert H. Grosvenor, director of the National Geographic Society, spearheaded the effort to establish Katmai as a national park or monument. Only an act of Congress can establish a national park, but a monument can be created either by presidential proclamation under the Antiquities Act of 1906 or by an act of Congress.

Griggs and Grosvenor entered into discussions with Stephen Mather, head of the National Park Service (NPS), and with Secretary of Interior Franklin Lane.

One pressing question nagged at all parties to the discussions, however. Would the smokes last? The answer to that question was of vital importance to the National Park Service and the President. The 1918 National Geographic expedition of Sayres and Hagelbarger was sent primarily to obtain measurements that would help answer that question. Finding the fumaroles in the same condition as they were the previous year, they concluded that the smokes were not dying out and said the Valley of Ten Thousand Smokes could be considered "a relatively permanent phenomenon."

Largely on the basis of these findings, the Valley of Ten Thousand Smokes was recommended by the National Park Service for designation as a national monument. President Woodrow Wilson signed the proclamation declaring the 1,700 square mile area surrounding the Valley of Ten Thousand Smokes as Katmai National Monument in 1918, just one year after the establishment of Mt. McKinley National Park, making Katmai the second oldest unit of the National Park system in Alaska.

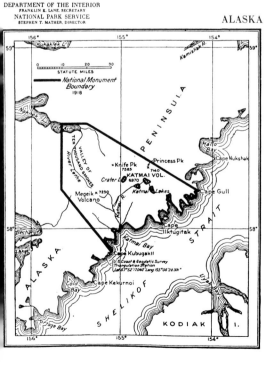

Katmai National Monument as established by the Proclamation of September 24, 1918. NATIONAL PARK SERVICE

The Struggle to Keep the Monument

Considerable opposition arose in Alaska to the formation of Katmai National Monument by those fearing it would lock the land up from development. The territorial governor Thomas Riggs, Jr. pleaded in 1918, "For the sake of the future of Alaska, let there at least be no more reservations without a thorough investigation on the ground by practical men and not simply on the recommendation of men whose interest in the Territory is merely academic or sentimental."

Having lost the battle to develop Katmai, Riggs declared in 1920 that "Katmai Monument serves no purpose and should be abolished." After Riggs, most of the territorial governors appreciated and supported the monument, recognizing it for its spectacular lake and mountain country. Nevertheless, the threat of development continued to loom over Katmai National Monument.

Katmai was expanded gradually by a series of presidential proclamations. In 1931, Herbert Hoover added Naknek Lake and extended the boundary to the north, increasing Katmai's size to 4,214 square miles. A proclamation in 1936 protected the rights of those who had been using the land since before the formation of the monument.

Katmai remained largely unvisited for many years and was administered from the Denali National Park office. Between 1918 and 1940, not one park service employee visited the monument, except the chief ranger of Denali who flew over in an airplane in 1937.

When Frank Been of the National Park Service and Victor Cahalane of the Biological Survey spent the summer of 1940 surveying Katmai by foot, boat, and plane, it marked a turning point in the management of the monument. They saw signs of poaching and illegal hunting and trapping everywhere. The Alaska Game Commission had already arrested fish and game violators that year, including Roy Fure, whose cabin still stands on the shore of Bay of Islands. Been and Cahalane recommended that the NPS take a more active role in protecting the resources of Katmai. Meanwhile, the smokes in the Valley of Ten Thousand Smokes had largely died out; the two men had counted only ten.

In 1941 the Territory of Alaska Department of Mines attempted to abolish the monument. The department had noted an area of great mineral potential between Mount Katmai and Kamishak Bay. It declared that, with the dying of the smokes, the justification for the monument was gone. Furthermore, the department added, the climate made the area unattractive to tourists. The drive was rebuffed by the National Park Service and, in 1942, Franklin D. Roosevelt added all islands within five miles of the Katmai coast to the monument.

With the coming of World War II, the military expanded its presence on the Alaska Peninsula, establishing bases in nearby King Salmon. Military personnel flocked to Katmai for recreation. They fished Katmai extensively, pulling thousands of trout from the lakes; they hunted and left trash behind. Responding to the increased use, in 1945, the National Park Service recommended a study to determine management needs. Funding was scarce, however, and no rangers or staff were assigned to the monument.

Katmai was again threatened in 1945-46 by commer-

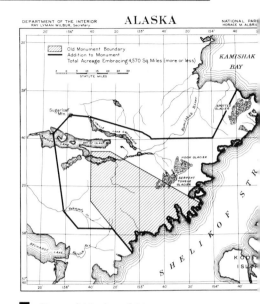

Katmai National Monument as enlarged by President Hoover's Proclamation of April 24, 1931.
NATIONAL PARK SERVICE

cial fishing and clamming operations that wanted to use Pacific coast land for fishing and processing operations. Commercial fishermen, territorial officials, chambers of commerce and individuals pressured the government, and a bill was introduced to the legislature to abolish the monument. One supporter of the measure stated that Katmai was "a barren place, devoid of all interest to tourists." The National Park Service found a compromise to the situation by stating that, although permits were required for the construction of onshore processing facilities, the monument boundaries ended at high tide line and no permit was necessary to fish offshore.

In 1947 people wanted to export pumice from Katmai for building materials in Anchorage saying, "Enterprise is the stability of the American nation, and no type of excavation, loading or hauling can in any way disfigure any part of this area." A bill enabling Congress to issue permits to excavate pumice was introduced in 1951 but was not enacted until 1954.

In 1950, yet another ambitious campaign to decrease the size of the monument was waged by trappers and fishermen who suffered in the low-return salmon run of 1949. The status of Katmai National Monument was firmly established by then, however, and threats to its borders were more easily averted.

Katmai Comes of Age

In 1950, an Alaskan entrepreneur, Ray Petersen, and his bush flying service, Northern Consolidated Airlines, saw the tourism potential of Katmai National Monument. That year they established two camps, Brooks Camp and Grosvenor Camp, and offered tourist packages from Seattle and Anchorage to Katmai. The National Park Service was by then able to dedicate more resources to the monument and, in the summer of 1950, the first seasonal ranger was stationed at Katmai.

Within three years, troubles of a new nature plagued the monument. By 1953, bears had begun to visit Brooks Camp, looking for food and garbage, and encountering humans. Biologists who visited the area that year noted the inevitability of the problems because the camp sat in the heart of the bears's natural fishing grounds. While visitors delighted in watching the brown bears, the bears learned bad habits in the open dumps used at the time. The incidents peaked in 1966 when a bear bit a man in the thigh and buttock as he slept in Brooks Campground, dragging the man ten feet before the bear could be chased off.

Park rangers urged adoption of a consistent bear management plan and, in 1967, the two open dumps in use at Brooks Camp were closed. In 1972 bears broke into numerous cabins in Brooks Camp, causing $21,000 in property damage. Little was done to manage the bears for several years until the monument was redesignated a national park.

Congress formed Katmai National Park in 1980 with the passage of ANILCA under President Jimmy Carter. The boundaries were extended from their 1969 position to encompass another one million acres, 308,000 acres of which were designated as national preserve. Of the total parkland, 3.4 million acres were declared wilderness.

With Katmai's change in status, the number of visitors grew, and the National Park Service intensified its management activities. The agency focused on potential bear problems in the Brooks River area. It built the second food storage cache at Brooks Campground in 1981. The dump on the Valley Road was removed in 1982. From then on, all trash was incinerated or removed from the park. Potential bear incidents near Brooks Falls were targeted next by building the bear view-

Fording Katmai River.
© NATIONAL GEOGRAPHIC SOCIETY

ing platform in 1982 and re-routing the Brooks Falls trail away from the river the following year.

The General Management Plan (GMP) was finalized in 1986; it outlined the principle mandates of the park: to provide protection of bears in their habitat; and to protect the cultural resources of the park. The GMP required the NPS to devise a Development Concept Plan (DCP) outlining how the park would be developed consistent with the mandates of the GMP. The process is ongoing as of this writing.

The NPS commissioned a study in 1988 to investigate the bear-human interactions in the Brooks River area. Conducted by Utah State University, the study looked at the impact of people on bears using the river. It concluded that some 40 percent of bears in the Brooks River area were altering their behavior or leaving the area altogether when humans were present.

In 1989, crude oil from the super tanker *Exxon Valdez*, which spilled 11 million gallons of oil in Prince William Sound 400 miles away, smeared the beaches of Katmai. The NPS realized at that time how little it knew of the coastal resources of the park and preserve. Since then, the NPS has speeded development of a research program to study the wildlife, vegetation, and other natural resources of Katmai.

As the boundaries of Katmai have changed during the 75 years since it was designated as a monument, so too has its mission and identity. Originally established to preserve the Valley of Ten Thousand Smokes, the park is probably known more widely today for the brown bears that live there. Another unique feature that has emerged is the rich cultural history of Katmai. From the deep lakes to the active volcanos, Katmai is a wild treasure. The continued preservation of this bountiful land is a statement of recognition of our deep connection with this world.

Part 2: INSIDE KATMAI

Rangers are on hand to greet you upon arrival at Brooks Camp, the center of park activities. (above) EDWARD BOVY / (below) JEAN BODEAU

Preceeding page:
Katmai caldera. USGS PHOTO BY AUSTIN POST

CHAPTER 9

Brooks Camp

Welcome to Brooks

Connected by regular flight service to King Salmon, Brooks Camp is the hub of many visitor's Katmai experience. Brooks Camp provides the easiest access to Katmai National Park and is the jumping off point for the Valley of Ten Thousand Smokes. Visitors can sleep under the trees in Brooks Campground or rent a cabin at Brooks Lodge.

Brooks Camp is nestled in the spruce-cottonwood forest between the pumice-lined shore of Naknek Lake and the marshy oxbow area of the Brooks River, world-renowned for its resident brown bear population. From the bear viewing platform at Brooks Falls, visitors can watch bears fishing and interacting in their own environment. People quickly develop an awareness of bears in Katmai. Bears fish the same rivers as anglers, they cruise the beach of Naknek Lake, and may even wander through camp on occasion.

A delicate relationship exists between humans and bears in Brooks Camp. It is governed by an etiquette which does not come naturally to most of us, and so the National Park Service has developed special guidelines and rules. It is critical that visitors understand the basis for the rules and follow them to ensure the safety of humans and bears. Anyone who violates a bear rule in Katmai may receive a citation. Chapters 2 and 12 focus on bears and appropriate behavior in bear country.

Brooks Camp was estab-

lished in 1950 as a fly-in fishing camp by Ray Petersen, an Alaskan aviation pioneer. Petersen and his bush flying company, Northern Consolidated Airlines, built four other lodges in the remote Katmai wilderness in addition to Brooks Camp. Brooks Camp was named after Dr. Alfred Hulse Brooks (1871-1924), who was head of Alaskan activities of the U.S. Geological Survey from 1903 until his death in 1924. At the time of his death, Brooks was considered the foremost expert on Alaska. Brooks's informative book, *Blazing Alaska's Trails*, was not finished or published until after his death.

Access

Most people take a commercial flight from Anchorage to King Salmon, then transfer to an air taxi for a 30-minute flight from King Salmon to Brooks Camp.

Anchorage - King Salmon

Airlines schedule daily flights between Anchorage and King Salmon from June through mid-September, leaving three to six times per day. Round trip fare in 1996 was $395, or $324 with 2-week advance purchase. Reservations can be made by calling Reeve Aleutian [(907) 243-4700], Alaska Airlines [1-800-426-0333], or Peninsula Airways [(907) 243-2323].

For Further Information

Katmai National Park and Preserve
P.O. Box 7
King Salmon Mall
King Salmon, AK 99613
(907) 246-3305
General park information and Brooks Campground reservations.

King Salmon Visitor Center
P. O. Box 298
King Salmon, AK 99613
(907) 246-4250
Joint operation of the U. S. Fish and Wildlife Service, National Park Service, Bristol Bay Borough and Lake & Peninsula Borough. Films, exhibits, information, and sales of books, maps and charts.

Alaska Public Lands Information Center
Old Federal Building
605 W. Fourth Ave, Suite 105
Anchorage, AK 99501
(907) 271-2737
Recorded information (907) 258-7275
Book sales and mail order sales available; information on public lands.

Katmailand Inc.
4700 Aircraft Dr.
Anchorage, AK 99502
(907) 243-5448 or 1-800-544-0551
Information about Brooks Lodge, Valley of Ten Thousand Smokes, tour, charter aircraft, and guiding services.

U. S. Geological Survey
Public Inquiries Office
4230 University Drive
Anchorage, Alaska 99508
(907) 786-7011
For topographic maps.

Barrier Free Access

Wheelchair-accessible accommodations are available at Brooks Camp. The lodge and one cabin have ramps; the shower has a grabber, seat, and detachable shower head. While the Brooks Falls trail would be extremely difficult for a wheelchair to navigate because of the roots, other wheelchair-accessible recreational opportunities include going to Brooks Lake, visiting the Valley of Ten Thousand Smokes, and taking canoe or boat trips.

King Salmon to Brooks Camp

Several air taxi services offer daily flights between King Salmon and Brooks Camp. Contact the park for a current list of concessioners. Round trip fare in 1996 was about $130. Private pilots should contact the park for regulations and guidelines concerning air traffic, and for navigational charts.

National Park Service Facilities

Park Visitor Center

Upon arriving, all visitors are required to proceed to the log cabin visitor center for park orientation by the National Park Service. Here you can buy books and post-cards,obtain free back-country permits, view an interac-tive bear video about bear behavior, and learn about the park interpretive services. The park offers interpretive services such as evening programs. Check the bulletin boards for times and topics.

Brooks Campground

Camping is free in the National Park Service campground, which is open year-round. Reservations are required from June through September. Information about reservations is available from the National Park Service at Katmai headquarters in King Salmon. Please notify the park of any changes in plans, such as late arrival or cancellation, or the entire reservation may be cancelled. Be sure to check in at the Brooks Camp Visitor Center upon your arrival. The campground's capacity is 60 campers per night. Campers are limited to seven nights per summer.

Campers should bring a camp stove to cook on. White gas is not permitted on airplanes; it may be purchased after arriving in Brooks Camp from Katmai Trading Post. Fires are allowed in the campground, but only dead and down wood may be burned. However, cooking over campfires is prohibited. Drinking water is provided only during the summer and fall.

Special rules are in place at Brooks Campground because of the bears. All food and garbage must be stored in the bear-proof buildings at the campground. Cooking is allowed only in designated areas, and no food or odorous items such as toothpaste, lip balm, or lotions are allowed in tents. Campers should know and adhere to the rules which are posted on the campground bulletin board.

The campground is an idyllic spot with purple wild geranium twining up through the grasses. Gray jays (aka Camp Robbers) hold vigil in the trees above picnic tables. Squirrels and red voles also share the campground. Fireweed, yarrow, tall Jacobs ladder, beachpea, and bedstraw thrive along the beach between the trees and the pumice.

Brooks Lodge.
EDWARD BOVY

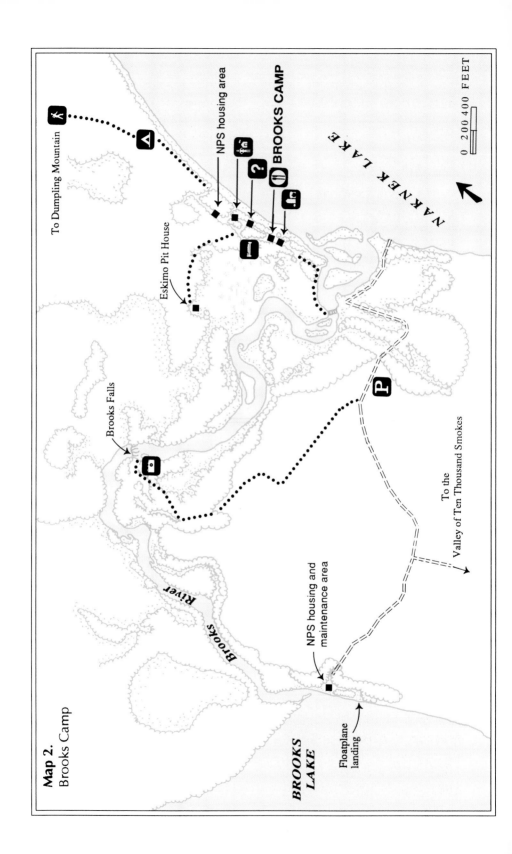

Map 2.
Brooks Camp

To Dumpling Mountain

NPS housing area

BROOKS CAMP

Eskimo Pit House

NAKNEK LAKE

0 200 400 FEET

Brooks Falls

Brooks River

BROOKS LAKE

NPS housing and maintenance area

Floatplane landing

To the Valley of Ten Thousand Smokes

Concession Facilities and Services

Brooks Lodge

Brooks Lodge has sixteen rooms and cabins, housing two-to four people each, with toilets, showers, heat, and electricity. In 1996, a cabin cost $260-$295 per night. The lodge is open from about June 1 through September. Stays are limited to three nights in a row; book your reservations early! Package tours from Anchorage are also available. The lodge serves three all-you-can-eat buffet-style meals every day; in 1996, breakfast was $10, lunch was $12 (sack lunch for $7), and dinner was $22. Children's meals cost less. The lodge has a bar and a lounging room with a big fireplace in the center, and picture windows with a view over Naknek Lake. All visitors to Katmai are welcome to patronize the lodge.

Other Visitor Services

A daily bus **tour to the Valley of Ten Thousand Smokes** leaves at 9 am and returns at about 4 pm. The tour takes visitors on the 23-mile (37-kilometer) dirt road out to the Three Forks Over-look cabin which overlooks the Valley. A trail descends from the cabin to the raging Ukak River that incises the massive ashflow sheet formed during the 1912 eruption of Novarupta. The bus waits at the cabin for several hours so visitors can hike down to the river. Advance reservations are recommended for the trip because it fills quickly. Cost in 1996 was $57 with lunch and $50 without lunch. Backpackers pay $30 each way; reservations are required for both legs of the trip. No lunch is provided for one-way passengers.

Katmai Trading Post sells sweatshirts, t-shirts, white gas, clothing, souvenirs, film, batteries, pop and candy, freeze-dried food, toothpaste and drugs, some fishing gear, and other miscellaneous items. Showers are available through the Trading Post; $4 in 1991 bought ten minutes of hot water, soap, and a towel. Guiding services for fishing, hiking, and boating are available. Flightseeing tours can be arranged at Brooks Camp.

Rentals available from Brooks Lodge include (1996 rates): canoes for $30/day or $5/hour (no advance reservations accepted); fishing equipment and waders; and bear proof food containers.

Hikes Near Brooks Camp

Hiking is not as popular in Brooks Camp as it is in other national park centers due in part to the ubiquity of brown bears and alder thickets. There are few hiking trails in the Brooks Camp area, unless you count bear trails, so most hiking is cross-country. I am not discouraging people from hiking, only reminding hikers to be ever-vigilant for bears and to expect to engage in serious bushwacking. There are four hiking trails in the Brooks area.

Native Barabara

Five to ten minutes down the trail from the auditorium is a *barabara*, a traditional Native dwelling, which has been reconstructed to demonstrate how the Natives of several thousand years ago lived.

Brooks Lake

A half-mile-long dirt road connects Brooks Camp with Brooks Lake to the west. The road begins on the other side of the bridge from Brooks Camp. The Brooks Falls trail branches off the north side of the road; slightly farther, the turnoff to the Valley of Ten Thousand Smokes veers off to the south. Across Brooks Lake you can see Mount Brooks and Dumpling Mountain. Several park service buildings sit at the end of the road on Brooks Lake.

Brooks Falls

The trail to Brooks Falls departs the north side of the road between Brooks Camp and Brooks Lake. The gentle trail winds through the mossy floor of the spruce forest to the bear viewing platform at Brooks Falls, a 10- to 15-minute walk from the road. The buff-colored ash of the 1912 eruption is visible in the upper portion of the soil profile beneath the humus.

Dumpling Mountain

The Dumpling Mountain trail begins in the campground. It climbs 1.7 miles to the overlook, a brisk 35-minute walk through moderately steep terrain. The trail winds through poplar and birch forest, with a grassy understory brimming with wildflowers such as fireweed, yarrow, geranium, bedstraw, and cow parsnip. Bear trails criss-cross the hiking trail so people should call or sing as they walk and be alert for bears. From the overlook, which is a bald knob of igneous rock, there are good views of Brooks River, the oxbow, Brooks and Naknek Lakes, Iliuk Arm, Mount Katolinat, and the Brooks Camp area.

The trail continues beyond the overlook up through rolling alpine tundra to reach the rounded summit of Dumpling Mountain about 1 1/4 hours later. During the summer, the tundra is dotted with bright pink Kamchatka rhododendron and other tiny wildflowers. The summit of Dumpling Mountain is four miles from the campground.

(right) **Visitors can reach the Valley of Ten Thousand Smokes by bus or truck.** *(below)* **The good old days, 1962.** (both) KATMAILAND, INC.

Photographing Bears

There are three major locations to photograph the bears: the viewing platform at Brooks Falls, the lower river platform and the beach near the campground.

The viewing platform lets you get as close as 20 feet to some of the bears. Many bears wait at the base of the platform for a fishing spot to open at the falls so you can get some excellent shots with a normal lens. In summer, the light is best at the falls from about 2 p.m. to 7 p.m. "Automatic" cameras will be strongly influenced by the bright sunlight reflecting off the waterfalls; remember, bears usually have dark coats and your camera can unintentionally silhouette them if you don't adjust your exposure. Take your light meter readings on mid-tone green vegetation on the far shore. Since space is limited on the viewing platform, park rangers will limit your stay when other people are waiting.

If this platform is crowded, try the lower river platform. Here you can see bears looking for fish in the lagoon or sleeping on the opposite shore or on an island. Don't forget to photograph the fish as they swim upstream. A polarizer will cut the glare from reflections off the water.

Bears walk up and down the beach so you can frequently see them from the campground. A nice bonus is to get one passing in front of a Naknek Lake sunset late in the evening.

But there is more to photograph besides bears! On your way to the falls, you can do some macro work on mushrooms and mosses in the forest and watch for snowshoe hares and spruce grouse. At the falls, look for harlequin ducks and a family of mergansers; 12 or more chicks may accompany their mother. Look for bear footprints on the beach. Magpies and gulls frequent the beach too, looking for fish scraps. Dumpling Mountain gives you a wonderful view on a clear day; watch out for moose along the trail.

Park rangers strictly enforce minimum bear viewing distances so bring a quality telephoto lens if you want good closeups. Take twice as much film as you think you will use; film speeds of 100 or 200 will likely be the most useful. Travel with a friend so one person can watch for bears while the other photographs. The single most important way you can improve your photos is to use a tripod with cable release.

–Edward Bovy

Kulik Lodge. JEAN BODEAU

CHAPTER 10

Other Lodges in the Park and Preserve

Angler's Paradise Lodges

Grosvenor Lake Lodge

Grosvenor Lake Lodge is a small fishing camp located between Grosvenor and Coville Lakes. According to the operator, Grosvenor is the "best kept secret in the sportfishing world." Its three intimate cabins with heat and electricity house a maximum of 6 people, with lounge and dining areas in separate buildings. Packages included airfare from Anchorage, lodging, meals and guide service.

Kulik Lodge

Located between Kulik and Nonvianuk Lake on private land in Katmai Park, Kulik Lodge is one of the most exclusive fly-in lodges in Katmai.

Kulik can accommodate up to 20 guests in cabins equipped with electricity, showers and toilets. Kulik has a log lodge and a sauna. The lodge provides daily fly-outs, transportation from Anchorage, lodging, meals and guide service.

For further information on these two lodges, contact:

Sonny Petersen
4700 Aircraft Drive
Anchorage, AK 99502
(907) 243-5448
800-544-0551

Enchanted Lake Lodge

Another of Katmai's exclusive fly-in fishing lodges, Enchanted Lake Lodge is located on private land on the south shore of Nonvianuk Lake within Katmai National Park.

Enchanted Lake Lodge accommodates up to twelve guests per week in cabins equipped with full bathrooms and electricity. The lodge provides daily fly-outs for guests as well as meals, cocktails, a sauna, guiding, and other amenities.

For further information contact:

> Dick Matthews
> October 16 - May 15
> 3222 West Lake Sammamish
>   Way S.E.
> Bellevue, WA 98008
> (206) 643-2172
>
> May 15 - October 15
> P.O. Box 97
> King Salmon, AK 99613
> (907) 246-6878

Battle River Wilderness Retreat

Battle River Wilderness Retreat is a rustic fishing lodge in the northern part of Katmai on Battle Lake. The Conways also conduct rafting/fishing trips on the Alagnak River starting from the "Hammersley Camp" cabins at the outlet of Nonvianuk Lake.

For further information contact:

> Tim and Wendy Conway
> 8076 Caribbean Way
> Sacramento, CA 95826
> (916) 381-0250
> (907) 243-5448

▌Kulik Lodge JEAN BODEAU

Grosvenor Lake Lodge cabins.
KATMAILAND, INC.

King Salmon

King Salmon is an airline and administration hub for the Alaska Peninsula. The dominant landmarks in King Salmon are the airport and the King Salmon Mall, where the Katmai National Park headquarters is located, as well as a bank and a travel agency. The mall is located to the right of and across the street from the airport. King Salmon has several restaurants a few stores that sell a limited selection of goods at fairly steep prices.

Naknek, located down the road on the Naknek River, is a key town in the Bristol Bay fishery.

There are several hotels in King Salmon; in 1991, they included the following:

King Ko Inn
Box 346
King Salmon, AK 99613
(907) 246-3377

Ponderosa Inn
Box 234
King Salmon, AK 99613
(907) 246-3444 or (907) 246-3360
Also offers fishing packages

Quinnat Landing Hotel
5520 Lake Otis, Suite 101
Anchorage, AK 99507
(907) 561-2310
Also offers fishing and Katmai
   packages

Eskimo Creek Lodge
(907) 246-3449

Fishing

Fishing Fever

Fishing fever runs epidemic in Katmai every summer, as it does throughout much of Alaska. Katmai offers boundless opportunities for fishing and even those who have rarely fished may catch the fever. Several lodges in Katmai cater specifically to anglers, and private guides are available throughout the region. A number of lodges outside the park fly in to Katmai for one-day or longer fishing excursions. Guides and power boats can be hired at Brooks Lodge, which also rents canoes.

Located in the heart of the Katmai lake country, the clear, tumbling **Brooks River** is known world-wide for its healthy rainbow trout population. It also boasts excellent grayling fishing and sometimes Dolly Varden and arctic char. Perfect for flyfishing, the river is shallow enough to wade from end to end and from side to side. To protect the population, only catch-and-release fishing is permitted for rainbow trout. Other fishing restrictions are discussed below and in current fishing regulations. Anglers will find the best rainbow trout fishing in lakes in early August, while in the rivers it is best right after the June 8 opening, before the salmon run begins, or in late August. When the salmon are running, trout fishing is difficult because the riv-

Southwest Alaska has lured fishermen for many years.
JAMES GAVIN

ers are choked with salmon and bears roam freely along the river.

Many people also fish the Brooks River for sockeye salmon. Huge runs of salmon swarm up the river from Bristol Bay from late June until the second or third week in July. A few silver salmon also run up the Brooks River, but not until late August and early September. The king (chinook) salmon run in the Brooks River is meager. A drawback to salmon fishing in the Brooks River is the abundance of brown bears and the potential for encounters with them.

Bay of Islands in Naknek Lake is a place to go for really big rainbow trout. In 1991, a 23-pound, 32-inch rainbow was pulled from these deep waters. They average about eight to 10 pounds from Bay of Islands. Lake trout can also be found in Naknek Lake, although by early July they have retreated to the depths and are rarely caught. Northern pike lurk in the reedy areas along the shores of Bay of Islands, and local legend tells of a haunted pike hole in the bay. **Brooks Lake** has lots of rainbow trout, although at three to four pounds they're not as large as in Naknek Lake.

Smaller lake trout also live in Brooks Lake.

Iliuk Arm is very silty since it is fed by the glacial Savonoski River, so fishing is poor. **Margot Creek** which drains into the arm is known for its Dolly Varden.

Lake Grosvenor has phenomenal fishing for rainbow, lake trout and arctic char. Says Perry Mollan, manager of Brooks Lodge, "It's awesome. When the salmon fry come down the river, lake trout start boiling the surface of the water like piranhas. You can actually see them jumping out of the water to eat the fry at mouths of any of the tributaries. The whole lake is excellent fishing."

Other areas in the park which are known for their fishing include the Moraine River in the north near Battle Lake, and American Creek. Outside the park, the **Alagnak River** is famous for rainbow trout and king salmon (see Chapter 15).

Equipment

Fishing conditions vary widely with fish weighing from two to 16 pounds. Many anglers bring two or more fly rod systems with matching lines to enable them to fish a vari-

KATMAILAND, INC.

ety of conditions. In addition to rod and reel, a pair of neoprene chest waders is recommended. Typical systems for Katmai might consist of:

For grayling, arctic char and rainbow trout:
Rod: 6 weight system
Lines: Weight forward floating line and a 10- to 20-foot fast sink tip line
Leaders: 2 pound to 6 pound spools
Reel: Exposed rim reel with 100 yards or more of backing capacity

For salmon and all freshwater fish:
Rod: 8 weight system, any kind of spinning rod or fly rod, a fighting butt might be helpful
Lines: Weight forward floating line with a fast sink tip 10 to 20 feet long; in fast water, a very fast sinking line may be helpful
Leaders: 6 pound to 12 pound or heavier
Reel: Reel should be compatible with the rod and have an adequate drag system or rim control with 150 to 200 yards of backing capacity

Flies

Most common fly patterns work in Katmai. Common flies recommended by anglers include: dry flies such as Adams, Royal Wulff, Humpy's, Elk Hair Caddis, and Irresistibles; in the spring, salmon smolt or fry patterns and sinking flies like Muddler Minnows, and bright streamers; Hare's Ears nymphs, Wooly Bugger, Black and Olive Marabou Muddlers, Polar Shrimp, and Egg Sucking Leach; in the fall, salmon egg patterns for trout; for sockeye, Coho, Green Marvel, and Sockeye John.

Other recommended equipment

Neoprene chest waders and boots
Needle nose pliers or hemostats
Quality raingear
Warm polypropylene or wool clothing

After the Catch: Unhooking and Releasing Fish

The treatment of fish by anglers is less than healthy. I've seen people pull fish out, unhook them, and kick them back in. I'd like to see anglers be really conscious of how they catch a fish and release it. I'd like to see them take the barbs off their hooks. An angler who keeps his line tight is not going to lose a fish by using barbless hooks.

> Bill Allan
> Avid angler and
> 1991 Brooks Campground
> Host

Fish grow slowly in the cold, relatively unproductive waters of Alaska. They continue to thrive in the rivers and lakes of Katmai in part because of catch-and-release fishing. Catch-and-release is required for rainbow trout on several streams and lakes for much of the year. Anglers are encouraged to practice catch-and-release for all freshwater species year-round. For the protection and health of the fish, please handle them carefully and gently.

<u>Handle a fish as little as possible</u>, keeping it under water. Avoid putting fingers in the delicate gills; these are the fish's lungs and are easily damaged. Do not squeeze the fish tightly or step on it, as this may damage its internal organs. Carry a needle-nosed pliers to help remove the hook; if it is badly hooked, it may be better to cut the line and leave the hook in the fish where enzymes might eventually dissolve it.

<u>Fish with barbless hooks</u> to decrease the hooking damage to the fish (and to the accidentally hooked hand). Once a fish is hooked, it rarely slips off even a barbless hook. Barbless hooks can be purchased or made by mashing the barbs on regular hooks with pliers.

JAMES GAVIN

Before releasing a fish, hold it facing into the current until it is reoriented. Release fish into calm water whenever possible. This will improve its chances of survival.

Fishing Regulations

A valid Alaska state fishing license must be in your possession when you are fishing. The current regulation book should be consulted for current regulations in each specific area. Some of the Brooks River regulations are summarized below. Fishing regulations and more information can be obtained through:

Alaska Department of Fish and Game
P.O. Box 3-2000
Juneau, AK 99802-2000
(907) 465-4270 Juneau
(907) 267-2218 Anchorage
(907) 246-3340 King Salmon

Brooks River Fishing Regulations
(summary)

Rainbow trout may not be kept. Rainbows caught from Brooks River and waters 1/4 mile into Naknek Lake must be released immediately.

Only unbaited, single-hook artificial lures may be used. Above the signs posted by the bridge, only unbaited single-hook artificial flies may be used.

No fishing is permitted within 100 yards of Brooks Falls.

If you hook a fish and someone else keeps it, that is still your daily limit.

Only fish hooked in the mouth are legal to keep.

Any fish kept must be placed in a plastic bag and carried immediately to the fish cleaning building. You may not store a fish on the river bank and continue to fish.

Move out of the river when a bear is approaching.

Make every effort to prevent bears from stealing fish from people.

CHAPTER 12

The Art of Living with Bears

Bear and Human Encounters

We are not aware of many of our encounters with bears, according to some bear experts. The bear usually detects us before we detect it, and it tries to avoid us. We can help the bear identify us by calling or singing loudly while we walk. We can allow our scent to precede us by walking in the downwind direction whenever possible. And we can behave in such a way that our actions do not encourage bears to become "problem bears."

Problem bears are nearly always bears that have learned two things: to be comfortable when they are close to people, becoming *habituated*; and to associate people with food, becoming *food conditioned*. Most of the art of living with bears is practicing behavior that prevents bears from acquiring these two traits. The rest of the art is having a strategy for averting human-bear encounters and, in the event of an encounter, knowing how to react.

Habituation and Food Conditioning

As visitors to Katmai, we see bears, sometimes as soon as we get off the airplane. At Brooks Camp, we may see them on the beach, in the river, walking between the cabins, or strolling through the campground. We get used to them quickly, feeling safe when we see their usually tolerant response to us. We grow bold enough to approach close for a better view or photo.

Likewise, bears become used to us. Our smell pervades their world: they see us at the viewing platform and on the trails; our cabins, tents, airplanes, and boats are everywhere in the Brooks River area. Some bears grow bold, cutting through camp or plopping down on the beach next to half a dozen anglers. They become habituated to us. We become habituated to them. We are all mutually habituated.

No problem ... No problem, that is, until somebody steps over the fluctuating line of acceptable behavior. If you get too close to a bear, or are perceived as threatening, the bear will nearly always respond. Respond how? Well, that depends. Like tapping a stranger on the shoulder, you don't know if he will turn around and kiss you, smile at you, hit you, or run. A bear's response depends on the animal, the circumstances of the encounter, and the mood of everyone involved. Bears usually react in one of four ways: leaving; ignoring you; warning you and giving you the opportunity to leave; or charging.

It is important to respect a bear's space. Invading it does far more than momentarily endanger the invader. It helps that bear grow accustomed to

being too near people, reducing the bear-only space it needs to maintain for its own comfort. Approaching a bear too closely enables it to enter human-only space more comfortably and easily. It doesn't take many close encounters to teach a bear that humans are less threatening than they previously thought. The bear that learns this will quickly be able to take its first step over the line of acceptable behavior.

Bears have far-reaching memories, particularly when it comes to food. If they are successful at getting food in a certain manner or location, they may not forget. A stolen fish, a sandwich, a fish carcass in a human-only zone, trash.... just one encounter with food has the potential to encourage an otherwise cooperative and "safe" bear to enter into human areas in search of food.

Habituation and food conditioning are a deadly combination. Unprovoked attacks by bears on humans have nearly all been inflicted by habituated, food-conditioned bears. Eight of the nine bear mauling deaths between 1967 and 1980 in Glacier, Banff, and Yellowstone National Parks were inflicted by habituated, food-conditioned bears. The ninth death was caused by a habituated bear with no known history of food conditioning. These deaths could probably have been avoided. The responsibility for food conditioning and habituation lies with people, not bears.

Bear in Mind...

Call, sing, or talk loudly while hiking to minimize your chances of surprising a bear. Bells and other noise-making devices are fine, but the human voice is much more effective; it carries farther and is more readily identifiable as human. Whistles are not a good idea; bears have been observed approaching rather than avoiding a whistle, possibly because it sounds like prey. Be especially alert when hiking through brushy areas or near streams where bears may be fishing.

If you see a bear at a distance while you are hiking, watch it carefully. If it does not see you, and you are heading in opposite directions, do not alert it to your presence. If it is coming your direction, change your course to avoid it and try to put yourself upwind of the bear.

If the bear shows an interest in you by looking, standing up, or approaching, help it to identify you and your party as humans: wave your arms over your heads; call loudly and calmly to the bear; back slowly away while calling; shift your position so that you are upwind of the bear, if possible. Anything you do to make you look larger will help; hold a jacket, daypack, or other items up over your head to make you appear larger.

If the bear charges, stand your ground. Most charges are bluffs.

Avoid looking the bear in the eyes, it may be interpreted as aggressive behavior.

Do not run from a bear; it could trigger a chasing instinct in the bear.

Keep your pack on; it will make you look bigger and afford some protection in the event of an attack.

If the bear attacks, drop to the ground, curl into a ball and cross your hands behind your neck to protect the neck and head, and play dead. Do not fight back against a brown bear.

In the Brooks Campground

Food Storage

All food, trash, and odorous items must be stored in the bear-proof storage cache. Odorous items include such things as: lip balm, toothpaste, toothbrush, pans, stoves, dishes, lotion, sunscreen, soap, perfume, and clothes that might smell like food. Space is very limited so do not bring excessive gear or large coolers.

Trash

Do not burn trash in the fire-rings because it never burns completely. Dispose of trash according to current park regulations.

Cooking Shelters

There are several cooking shelters in the campground. To keep the food-zone small, cooking is allowed only in the shelters or immediately in front of them. Please do not use the shelters to store belongings or to socialize except when handling food. There are a limited number of shelters that all campers use. After cooking and eating, please clean up and vacate the shelter so another party can use it. Do not leave food or cooking utensils in the shelters unattended.

Washing Dishes and Brushing Teeth

A spigot in front of the food caches provides potable drinking water. Before washing dishes, scrape all leftover food into a trash bag — every noodle, every last grain of rice. I like to put hot water in my bowl and drink the dishwater as "tea." After the pots and bowls are scraped as clean as possible, wash them with water. Pour dishwater out near the spigot, perhaps kicking a shallow hole in the gravel to pour the water into. Likewise, when brushing teeth, try to minimize the amount of toothpaste-scented water by using only a little toothpaste. Baking soda toothpaste or tooth powder might be a wise choice for bear country. Spit near the spigot after brushing teeth, possibly into a shallow hole to be covered over with gravel.

Do not wash with soap in the campground; odors can attract bears. The lodge has shower and sink facilities available for camper use.

Bears are everywhere around Brooks Camp and often use the beach by the campground as a highway to the Brooks River. JAMES GAVIN

Cleaning Fish

It is illegal to clean fish in the campground. At Brooks Camp, fish cleaning is allowed only inside the fish cleaning building or some other enclosed building.

Bear in the Campground!

The campground is designated as human-only space. If a bear approaches or enters the campground, back off and gather other campers together. Do not approach the bear. Be sure the bear-proof caches are closed and secured. If the individual bear is at least fifty yards away, or a family or group of bears is 100 yards away, and four or more campers are grouped together, the people might wave their arms and call loudly to the bear, telling it to stay out of the campground. If the bear is closer than these distances, back slowly away, calling loudly to the bear.

Around Brooks Camp

The Bear Highway

Bears have the right-of-way on the beach of Naknek Lake. If you see a bear on the beach, leave it alone. Do not chase it away. Before walking on the trail between the campground and the visitor center, which parallels the beach, look both ways on the beach. If a bear is along this stretch, or approaching it, change your plans. Wait until the bear is no longer on the beach, or make a wide detour through the woods.

Walking on Trails

Bears roam everywhere in Brooks Camp. Visitors should be prepared to meet bears outside their cabins and on the trails. The best precaution is to be constantly aware and watching for bears. Talk loudly or sing when walking on trails, unless in the immediate camp vicinity during daylight hours. Do not carry food or trash with you (except to the trash storage area), and save those fragrant perfumes, lotions, and sunscreens for town.

Stay at least fifty yards from all bears, and at least 100 yards from sows with young. If you see a bear nearby, point it out to others so they can adjust their actions accordingly.

While Fishing

Anglers interact with bears frequently and closely. They fish alongside bears in the river and compete with them for fish. Furthermore, the solitary nature of fishing means that the angler may be alone for an encounter. Anglers should take steps to avoid an encounter with a bear, but be prepared to react intelligently when a bear comes. Bear encounters are almost inevitable for anglers on the Brooks River.

Be alert while fishing, watching constantly for bears. Do not listen to a Walkman. Watch other anglers who may see a bear when you don't, and warn others when you see a bear. Stop fishing and start moving out of the water when you see a bear. Bears can move quickly in the water. Some judgement is needed on this matter; the objectives are to prevent bears from associating anglers and fish and, to allow bears, especially shy ones, access to the river for fishing.

If you have a fish on the line when a bear is nearby, break the line immediately.

As soon as you catch a fish that you intend to keep, bring it directly to the fish cleaning building. Do not store fish on shore.

UNDER NO CIRCUM- STANCES SHOULD A BEAR GET A FISH FROM AN AN- GLER. This encourages bears and could make fishing dan- gerous for years to come.

While Photographing

Use restraint while photo- graphing bears. Many people, when they have a camera in their hands, are inclined to approach bears too closely. This contributes to the unde- sirable process of habituating the bear to being too close to humans.

Juvenile bear on the Naknek Lake Beach.
JAMES GAVIN

CHAPTER 13

The Art of Camping Softly

Walking Lightly on the Land

All of us who head for the mountains, valleys and rivers love the earth. We revel in the wild beauty and feel renewed from even a short day outing. We care about the land and the water, and try to protect them. Yet good intentions don't always lighten our impact on the land as much as they could, and common sense sometimes falls short. Over the years, experienced backcountry travelers and educators have examined activities and impacts of humans in the wild. They have developed guidelines for living and moving in the backcountry

that can help us minimize our disturbance to the land and impact to the creatures who live there. Some suggestions for camping lightly are included below.

Fires versus Stoves

Use a backpacking stove rather than a fire for cooking. In addition to the blackened scars they leave, campfires deplete wood resources and contribute to the degradation of campsites. If you **do** decide to have a fire, remember that the best fires are those that are difficult to see the next day. Choose the fire site carefully, building the fire on mineral soils with no vegetation. If you assemble a fire circle, be sure to take it apart before leaving the campsite. Keep the fire small: a small fire can

| The Valley of Ten Thousand Smokes and Mount Griggs.
EDWARD BOVY

be just as enjoyable as a huge fire, and will burn less wood, be safer, and leave a smaller scar. Build fires only in areas where firewood is plentiful. Clean the fire scar up before leaving camp, scattering any ashes that remain, disassembling rocks arranged for the fire, and spreading gravel or soil over the burn scar.

Trash

Pack it in, pack it out. The best way to reduce your outgoing trash load is to watch what you bring in. Remove excess packaging before leaving town and cook food portions so no leftovers remain. Do not scatter or bury leftovers, it will draw the bears in and teach them to associate people and food. If you see trash left by others as you hike, please pack it out along with your own.

Sanitation

The main things we're trying to do with human waste are to keep it from polluting water, prevent anyone from finding it, and maximize its rate of decomposition. In Katmai, the best way to dispose of your feces is probably to dig a cathole, a small hole at least four to six inches deep and at least 200 feet from the nearest water. Burn toilet paper, carry it out, or don't even use it. Carry all tampons and pads out, storing used ones with the food and handling them in a similar manner as food waste.

Choosing a Campsite for Minimum Impact

Most of our time on a backcountry trip is spent in the campsite and most of the impacts occur there. There are no designated campsites in Katmai except Brooks Campground, so virtually all camping involves selecting a pristine campsite. A popular backcountry camp area in Katmai is the Valley of Ten Thousand Smokes, a unique camping environment, to be sure. Indeed, it is much like the surface of the moon and is fairly resilient to trampling. Nevertheless, following a couple of guidelines will help minimize the impact at campsites.

When a "frequently used campsite" exists, use it. It is better to concentrate impacts in one area than to spread them out over several sites. The National Outdoor Leadership School says, "Although almost all campsites sustain noticeable damage when camped on more than one or two nights every year, after a certain amount of camping, further use doesn't have much added effect. Frequently used campsites are affected far more by what you do when you're there than by how many times you're there." [1]

When you camp in a pristine area, consider these factors in choosing your location:

•Camp on stable surfaces without vegetation to avoid compacting soil and damaging the plants. In the Valley of Ten Thousand Smokes, avoid camping in the fragile warm spring areas;

•Camp away from water sources to avoid encountering and disturbing animals and to minimize the potential for water pollution;

•When you break your pristine camp, camouflage it as much as possible so other campers will not be tempted to use the same location. Replace rocks you moved from your tent site or cooking area. Rake flattened vegetation up-right again, and cover any scuffed areas with some duff. And, of course, leave it at least as clean as you found it.

Off-Trail Hiking

Except for a few hikes in the immediate vicinity of Brooks Camp, all of the hiking in Katmai is off-trail. Try to spread footprints out whenever possible. When hiking in a group, hike next to each other rather than single file to avoid creating new trails. Don't build cairns, blaze trees, or leave messages for other members of your group. This is a form of pollution that may detract from others' sense of wilderness. Choose routes across stable, non-vegetated surfaces when possible, avoiding fragile and wet zones. On steep terrain, follow the most gentle routes and walk on rocks and snow or ice rather than vegetation. Descend scree slopes slowly, since jumping can greatly accelerate erosion on these slopes.

(1) Excerpted from *Soft Paths* by the National Outdoor Leadership School, ©1988, reprinted with permission from Stackpole Books.

HUBBARD COLLECTION, SANTA CLARA UNIVERSITY ARCHIVES

"We therefore fell back on the most primitive of all
means of transportation — man-backpacking."

Robert F. Griggs
National Geographic Society

CHAPTER 14

Into the Wilderness

Into the Wilds with a Map and No Trail

A vast backcountry surrounds the tiny peopled core of Katmai. It is a backcountry as diverse as glacial icefalls and rugged sea coast, as deep, clear lakes and dry, alpine tundra. Backcountry explorers will find a Katmai that is trail-less and wild, where the wind howls across bare rock and brown bears are a certainty. Not a land for the timid or unprepared, Katmai beckons to those who find rewards in the mountains, forests, and rivers.

People have hiked or boated in many areas of the park throughout the years. Rather than describe specific routes in this book, which might encourage overuse of some areas at the exclusion of others, I'm suggesting that people pull out a map to see which areas summon them.

While the Valley of Ten Thousand Smokes is the most commonly hiked backcountry area, and the Savonoski Loop and Bay of Islands are favorite boating areas, the possibilities for backcountry travel are limited only by imagination, experience, and time. Nearly every area in the park and preserve is accessible by air taxi.

One could spend several weeks exploring within the Valley of Ten Thousand Smokes itself. There are volcanos to climb and volcanic features to explore. From the Valley, a number of other areas can be easily reached. The Buttress Range, Windy Creek, and the Knife Creek drainage are adjacent to the Valley.

Angle and Takayofo Creeks, underlain by frozen ground as they drop to Becharof Lake and National Wildlife Refuge to the southwest of the Valley, are home to large herds of caribou. The snowy volcanos of the Kejulik Mountains and the Aleutian Range — Trident, Katmai, Mageik, Griggs, Martin, and others — rise up to the south. Beyond the Katmai Pass lie Katmai Lakes, Katmai Canyon, the Mageik Landslide, and the Barrier Range.

The stony batholiths and high alpine tundra of the Walatka Mountains, up north by Kulik and Battle Lakes, entice hikers into their midst.

The Pacific Katmai coast, with fingering fiords such as Amalik, Kinak, and Kukak Bays, is home to brown bear as well as seal, whale and sea otter. Rarely visited, except by commercial fishermen, the outer coast is intriguing for sea kayaking.

Mount Douglas (7063 feet), Mount Denison (7606 feet), and other snowy volcanos challenge mountaineers.

Boaters can try the Alagnak River, the Ukak River, American Creek, and the outer coast.

The list is endless... So, as you plot your trip to Katmai, if you decide to venture into the backcountry, let the map inspire you.

Backcountry Permits

Backcountry permits are not required in Katmai National Park and Preserve. However, they are strongly recommended for the safety and protection of hikers and can be obtained at the visitor center in Brooks Camp or by mail from park headquarters. People traveling out of King Salmon to park destinations other than Brooks Camp can get permits from park headquarters in King Salmon.

Weather and Gear

Ask anyone who has hiked in the Valley of Ten Thousand Smokes to summarize the weather in one word, and they will nearly always say **WIND**. Winds stirred up in the Gulf of Alaska may reach 60 miles per hour in a matter of minutes as they blast across Katmai Pass. The winds scour the Valley of Ten Thousand Smokes, churning the fine ash particles into dust storms that reach to the stratosphere and hurl pumice through the air. A sturdy wind-resilient self-supporting tent is essential for campers in the Valley of Ten

Thousand Smokes. On occasion, even sturdy tents won't hold up to the wind. Some people wear goggles for protection against the pumice and dust storms.

Summer weather in Katmai is pleasant, with frequent rain and drizzle. Summer high temperatures range up to about 65 degrees and occasionally higher, while lows do not generally drop much below 50 degrees. More rain falls on the south side of the

Aleutians than on the north side; Brooks Lake receives only 15 inches of precipitation per year, a desert compared to Kodiak, which averages 54 inches annually, including snow.

The weather in Katmai can change quickly and without warning, turning from scorching sunshine to savage storm, so hikers must be prepared for anything. Adequate raingear and plenty of warm clothing are essential, including hat, gloves, polypropylene or wool clothing, windgear and pile jackets. Avoid down-filled clothing. Hypothermia is always a possibility when wet conditions and cool temperatures are the norm. Know what to do.

River Crossings

Hikers in Katmai will undoubtedly have to cross rivers on foot. Katmai's rivers are cold, swift, and powerful. Some are glacially fed, thick with silt, and ice-cold. Water levels can change markedly within an hour as glacial meltwater or rainfall drain into the rivers. The rivers are likely to be lower very early in the morning when glacial runoff is at a minimum.

Crossing the Ukak River below Three Forks. EDWARD BOVY

Hikers should cross with the utmost caution, being careful to select the best possible crossing location and following safety guidelines. Some people carry a pair of tennis shoes for river crossings. I prefer to cross in my boots, taking off socks and removing insoles before crossing. I save my tennis shoes for camp since my boots always seem to get wet anyway. Wear what you would want to be wearing should you fall in: polypropylene long underwear and an extra shirt. Pack important items like sleeping bags and cameras in plastic bags before crossing.

Bears in the Backcountry

Bears are everywhere in the backcountry of Katmai. Hikers must do everything in their power to avoid encounters with bears and to prevent

Tips for crossing rivers safely

- Scout the river before crossing to find the best possible place;
- Cross at the widest part of the river, where the water will likely be the shallowest and slowest. Throw a rock into the current to help judge the depth of the water in a silty river;
- Choose an area with many braids, if possible;
- Cross at a straight portion of the river, midway between bends, rather than at the bends where the current may have created deep trenches on the inside curve;
- Some people carry a stick to probe the bottom as they cross and to help balance;
- Unfasten the waist belt of your backpack before crossing so you can take your pack off quickly if you fall;
- Hold hands with your friends as you cross, having larger people walk upstream to help reduce the force of the current on smaller people;
- Cross facing upstream for greater stability.

bears from obtaining human food. Bears are not as common in the Valley of Ten Thousand Smokes as they are in other areas of the park, but their tracks are observed there every year. Furthermore, good visibility in the Valley reduces the possibility of chance encounters. Nevertheless, campers in all areas of Katmai should use extremely good judgment in bear matters. Chapters 2 and 12 of this book also address bears.

Bear Tips for the Backcountry

Do not camp on animal trails, or close to a water source that might be used by animals. Sleep in a tent rather than in the open; it makes you appear larger.

Separate food and sleeping areas by distances of at least 100 yards. Cook and store food downwind of the tent so bears that smell food and approach will encounter the food before the tent. The National Park Service recommends storing food in a location other than the cooking area, with cooking, storage, and tenting areas forming a triangle. Hang the food high in a tree, if trees are present. Store all trash, cosmetics, toothpaste, lip balm, used tampons (recommended over pads for camping in bear country), and other odorous items with the food.

Keep all food activities and areas fastidiously clean. Let not one grain of rice nor one drop of soup fall onto the ground. Scrape pots and dishes before washing them, and put any leftover food or scrapings into the trash.

Bear-resistant food containers are recommended. They are durable plastic cylinders that bears generally will not break into. They can be rented at Brooks Lodge or purchased from REI in Anchorage. Keep all food inside the containers until needed. Be prepared to put the partially cooked food into the container if a bear comes.

Wash your hands after handling food. Do not wipe your hands on clothing when handling food, and avoid sitting downwind of cooking food.

Backpacking in and Beyond the Valley of Ten Thousand Smokes

Maps

The Mt. Katmai *1:250,000* U.S.G.S. section map shows all of the Valley of Ten Thousand Smokes extending from Brooks Camp to Shelikof Strait. Hikers will probably want to have Mt. Katmai B-4, B-5, and A-4 *1:63,360* quadrangle maps (inch to the mile), at a minimum, for backpacking in the Valley of Ten Thousand Smokes. In addition, Mount Katmai and Crater Lake are shown on Mt. Katmai B-3, and Katmai Lakes, Katmai Canyon and the Barrier Range are shown on Mt. Katmai A-3. Going to the west, Angle Creek and Mount Martin are on Mount Katmai A-5 and A-6. All maps are available from the U.S.G.S. or the Public Lands Information Center in Anchorage. See page 117 for addresses.

Approaching the Valley of Ten Thousand Smokes

There are two approaches into the Valley of Ten Thousand Smokes from the Three Forks Overlook where the bus drops most people off (some people opt to walk the 23-mile (37-kilometer) road to the Valley).

Windy Creek is the traditional approach. To enter the Valley via Windy Creek, follow the road about 1/4 mile back from the Overlook Cabin. A trail descends to the left (south), dropping through shrubs and grasses to Windy Creek, which must be forded. On the other side of Windy Creek, the usual route is to climb onto the ashflow and skirt around the south and east sides of the Buttress Range. Bears may browse on the flanks of the Buttress Range so hikers should be alert. The trail fades once it reaches the Valley of Ten Thousand Smokes. A couple of indentations in the Buttress Range provide water and shelter from the wind. One frequently used camping spot approximately six miles from the trailhead is known as Six-Mile.

The other route into the Valley is to cross the Ukak River below Three Forks Overlook and walk up Knife Creek or the center of the Valley. The bridge across the Ukak River was destroyed by high water several years ago. Nevertheless, it is possible to jump across the river in some places near the bottom of the trail when water levels are low. For hikers wishing to approach Mount Griggs directly, this is the usual route. Hikers should exercise caution when jumping these rivers; a fall into the river gorge would almost undoubtedly be fatal.

The River Lethe

The River Lethe incises the ashflow in a twisting churning three-dimensional course unlike other earthly rivers. You can't see it until you're on top of it, but its roar travels far on the Valley winds. Griggs named the river after the River Lethe which flowed through hell in Greek mythology.

The River Lethe in the Valley of Ten Thousand Smokes can be crossed safely at just a few locations.

NATIONAL PARK SERVICE

There are two ways to cross the River Lethe: by jumping, or by finding a place to wade. In spots, the ashflow engulfs the river so completely that its only surface expression is a gap narrow enough to step or jump across. Most of the jumping spots are located slightly south of the north end of Baked Mountain. In other spots, the river emerges from its canyons for a few hundred feet, spreading across the ash in a wide river shallow enough to wade across. One such ford is located just south of Six-Mile.

In June, snowbridges across the narrower parts of the canyons may tempt you to cross to save time. This is not recommended as the snow can collapse in an instant.

Baked Mountain

Baked Mountain is interesting to hikers primarily because of the old geology research cabins located on the east side of the north ridge. The ramshackle cabins are rustic, but they are open to hikers and can provide a respite from the blasting winds and horizontal rains that occasionally visit the Valley.

There is no water source at the cabins, except for several water jugs that are kept inside. The jugs are filled from nearby snowmelt or rainfall sources, to which directions are normally left in the cabin. Visitors who use water should leave the jugs at least as full as they found them.

The Baked Mountain cabins are a long one day hike from the Overlook Cabin. Many of the prominent features in the Valley can be visited on day hikes from the cabins. Hikers can go virtually anywhere in and around the Valley of Ten Thousand Smokes, when equipped with a map, a bit of prudence, and appropriate gear. Novarupta is two to three hours from the cabins; Katmai Pass is a few hours farther.

The summit of Baked Mountain, where well-preserved fossils of the Naknek Formation are found, is an hour or two round-trip from the cabins. Some people base much of their trip out of the Baked Mountain cabins, although when the weather cooperates, there are far nicer places to camp. Cabin log book entries date back several years and are entertaining to read.

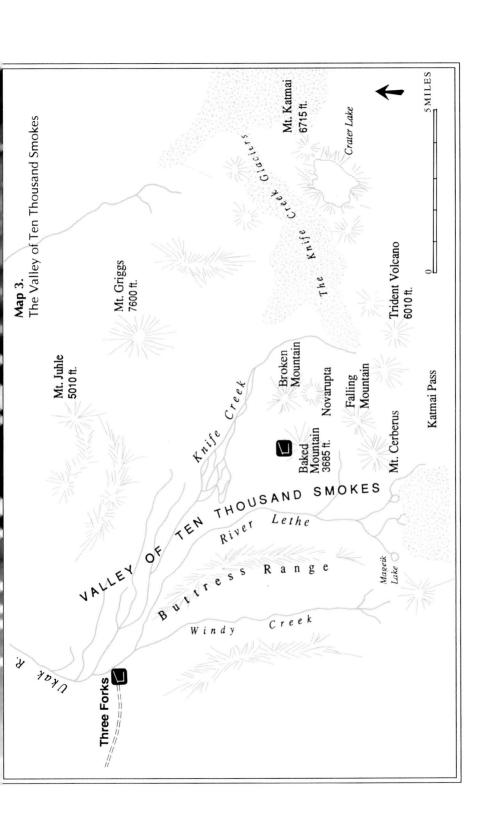

Map 3.
The Valley of Ten Thousand Smokes

Mt. Juhle
5010 ft.

Mt. Griggs
7600 ft.

Mt. Katmai
6715 ft.

Crater Lake

The Knife Creek Glaciers

Broken
Mountain

Novarupta

Falling
Mountain

Trident Volcano
6010 ft.

Baked
Mountain
3685 ft.

Mt. Cerberus

Katmai Pass

Knife Creek

VALLEY OF TEN THOUSAND SMOKES

River Lethe

Buttress Range

Mageik Lake

Windy Creek

Ukak R.

Three Forks

5 MILES

0

Thoughts from Baked Mountain

The cabins at Baked Mountain offer a place of refuge from some of Katmai's fickle moods. Few can resist trying to express their feelings after having traveled into the heart of the Valley of Ten Thousand Smokes.

Now I know what heaven looks like! Believe it or not, it's this pillbox of a cabin, welcome shelter from fierce elements, powerful wind gusts flinging themselves over the saddle between Baked and Broken mountains and driving rain.

Christian Basker
Vienna, Austria
1988

The best description of the interior portion of the valley is a "moonscape." I have observed no visible forms of life here other than the snow bunting. The air is permeated with acrid odor of sulfur and is only overpowered by the odor of my socks which my fellow cabin tenants claim is quite strong.

Pat Powell
Trinidad, Colorado
1982

With phasers on stun we flogged our way across the lunar landscape while getting sand-blasted by 30-40 m.p.h. winds. Two guys made it across the valley in the opposite direction in one fifth the time it took us. They appeared to be as close to human flying as possible. Now at the cabin my teeth are semi-professionally cleaned but my eye-glasses look like etched glass. Totally bizarre kind of place. But not nearly as bizarre as Bethel, Alaska.

Jill McLean
Bethel
1989

Earthquake! Three vibrations rolled across the cabin ground as I eyed the hammer and pulaski directly above my eyes threatening to give me a backcountry lobotomy. Not a pretty thought. In the morning we headed over to Mageik Lakes — incredible! Go visit them. High black cliffs, waterfalls and placid turquoise waters with glaciers spilling on all sides. Neat sandstone canyon at west Mageik outlet. Dust devils danced alongside shafts of sunlight on the valley floor in the evening.

Charlie Seard
1989

Beautiful weather the past few days. Clear skies, warm temperatures and light winds. Saw many animal tracks — caribou, fox, wolverine, wolf and bear (big!). Wolf tracks very recent and headed toward the pass. Bear tracks in the pass. No one here but me. A truly spectacular place — Mars, Venus, Earth, Heaven, Hell — all in one. Spent the last five hours simply watching and feeling the whole place change and change again. Red sunset in the west and rainbow in the east.

Michael Harding
Port Angeles, Washington
1989

After spending careful hours of contemplation, I chose a narrow gorge in which to jump the River Lethe. I fought a 30-knot headwind and driving rains yesterday to make it to the shack in eight hours. The river was way up and after one feeble attempt to ford and finding the bottom was quicksand I backed out and searched for the spot to jump. After the tragic loss of our Swiss camper this summer, I was

confronted with a respect, perhaps fear, of this river. Totally drenched I arrived around 8 p.m.

I am now being deafened by the pumice pounding on the windows. I can barely hear myself write. The winds must be blowing 50 to 60 m.p.h. Rain, wind and pumice, a delightful combination; it's hell. The wind is blowing so hard, small chunks of pumice and sand are being forced through a tiny crack in the window and are landing on the table. One can't even exit the cabin without being completely plastered with the stuff. It's going to be a long night.

Andy Fisher
1989

The Valley of Ten Thousand Smokes will change; it is not a valley of smokes anymore and one time it will not be very different at all from the other valleys in the monument. What looks like devastation and ruin at first sight really is creation. In nature nothing is destroyed, things are only changed and no condition is better or worse than it was before. That is what I learned again here, as in many other places on this continent.

Aljos Farjon
Netherlands
1980

Mageik Lakes

The milky blue Mageik Lakes at the base of Mount Mageik were formed when hot ash landed on the glaciers during the 1912 eruption of Novarupta. The lakes have now merged into one large lake. They are reached by following the green flanks of the Buttress Range south from Windy Creek, staying on the west side of the River Lethe. Desert-like canyons and "badlands" features rise on the southeast side of the lake and the area is good for camping. The river crossings between Mageik Lakes and Novarupta are fairly easy.

Novarupta

Latin for *newly erupted*, Novarupta is the name Robert Griggs bestowed on the vent of the explosive eruption of 1912. Griggs realized that Novarupta was a significant vent in the eruption, although he did not understand that it was the primary one. The Novarupta caldera is more than half a mile (one kilometer) in diameter, stretching between the blasted sides of Broken and Falling Mountains.

Novarupta dome, a fractured hill of ropy pumice, sits on a plateau between these two mountains. The fractured pile of rock is the final ooze of lava from the eruption. A tephra ring surrounds the lava dome and forms a prominent hill northeast of it known as the Turtle. The top of the Turtle is sliced by grabens, shallow vertical faults and blocks that have dropped and uplifted relative to each other. According to the most recent theory, an intrusion of magma beneath the tephra uplifted the Turtle.

Active fumaroles steam on the side of Novarupta, and some warm spring areas form bright green oases near it in the desert-like environment of the Valley. Please respect the plants in these areas; do not camp on or trample them.

Katmai Pass

The infamous Katmai Pass, which lies behind Mount Cerberus, is a destination for most hikers in the Valley of Ten Thousand Smokes. But why stop at the pass? Beyond the pass, reddish-black lava flows creep down the mountain over the pumice, reminders of the area's most recent volcanic eruption, Trident Volcano in 1953-68. Warm water seeps from beneath the lava flows, giving rise to red mineral creeks and lush pools surrounded by yellow monkeyflower. Observation Mountain blocks the view to Shelikof Strait but, around it lies access to the upper Katmai River, Katmai Canyon, and Katmai Lakes.

Katmai River, which was the historic route over the pass, changed dramatically after the 1912 eruption. The National Geographic party led by Robert Griggs in 1915 saw large trees snapped off at the ground, high water marks 25 feet (7.6 meters) above the then-still-high river level, and a water-transported boulder that they estimated at 150 tons. They deduced that a catastrophic and instantaneous flood had recently occurred, but were puzzled about its origins.

Apparently, an ash landslide dam had burst above Katmai Lakes, spilling the waters of a 950-acre lake down the canyon. The water rushed down the valley with 500 feet (150 meters) of head, attaining speeds of 100 feet (30 meters) per second. Today, in part because of this flood, the Katmai River is treacherous with quicksand, thick with alders, and Katmai village no

longer exists. Hikers planning to follow this route must arrange for a pick-up or dropoff, or plan to walk both ways across the pass.

Mount Katmai

The three-peaked Mount Katmai, which dominated the skyline before the 1912 eruption, collapsed under its own weight when the magma chamber beneath it was emptied during the eruption. The mountain's collapse created a spectacular caldera that is steep, more than a thousand feet deep, and ice-encrusted. Glaciers began forming almost immediately, the only glaciers in the world whose exact age is known, and the caldera is now glacier-rimmed. A turquoise blue lake rests in the bottom of the caldera and is filling at the rate of about six feet (two meters) per year. Despite predictions that the lake will overflow, it probably will not because the fractured walls of the caldera will drain the water before it overflows.

Hikers who climb Mount Katmai should be experienced at glacier travel and come equipped with rope, ice-axe, and rescue equipment at a minimum, and use caution when crossing the glaciers.

Knife Creek Glaciers

The Knife Creek Glaciers blanketed the slopes of Mount Katmai before the eruption. When Mount Katmai collapsed, the glaciers were cut off from their source and buried under a thick layer of ash. They have become stagnant since then and hardly look like

Paddling in Naknek Lake.
NATIONAL PARK SERVICE

ice. Hikers in the Valley like to explore the glaciers and they are used as an access route to reach Mount Katmai.

Trident Volcano

As its name implies, Trident Volcano has three jagged peaks, at least one of which can be ascended without crossing glaciers. Its eruptions during the years 1953 through 1968 were the most recent in Katmai.

Mount Griggs

Mt. Griggs is caked with ash from the 1912 eruption; it is difficult to tell that the mountain is really covered with snow. Nested craters formed by three successive eruptions are found at the top of the volcano. Mount Griggs can be climbed without glacier climbing equipment.

Mount Mageik

Glacier climbing equipment is needed to climb icy Mount Mageik and reach the bubbling green crater lake. Sulfuric acid steam rises up from the lake, the water of which has an acidity of pH 1. Although the water is only 70°C, the lake bubbles as gases rise up through it. Gases drifting around the lake could be dangerous and hikers should avoid inhaling them.

Other Wilderness Trips

Paddling the Savonoski Loop

The Savonoski Loop is an 86-mile (138-km) navigable circuit through the largest freshwater lakes in the national park system. Paddlers will traverse deep clear lakes surrounded by lush boreal forest and mountains on this four- to 10-day trip.

The Bay of Islands is a favorite fishing and camping area and is itself a paddling destination.

A one-mile portage trail connects Naknek Lake to Grosvenor Lake. It begins in Bay of Islands next to Roy Fure's old trapping cabin. The cabin was renovated by the National Park Service and a ranger is stationed there during the summer.

From the other side of the portage, the loop continues the length of Grosvenor Lake to its outlet at the southeast end. A Class I river flows into the braided Savonoski River and finally into Iliuk Arm of Naknek Lake.

Bears are common along the entire route, but especially along the Savonoski River. **Do not camp along the Savonoski River.**

The weather can change quickly, stirring up impressive waves in a matter of minutes. Boaters should always keep an eye on the sky and paddle close to shore so they can land if the water becomes rough. The north side of Iliuk Arm is steeply cliffed so paddlers might prefer to stay on the south side of the arm for ease of landing.

Canoes can be rented from Brooks Lodge, but no advance reservations are accepted. Bear-resistant food containers are also available for rental from the lodge and are highly recommended.

Maps needed for the trip: Mt. Katmai B-5, C-4,-5,-6.

Boat-Accessible Hikes Near Brooks Camp

Mount La Gorce, Mount Katolinat, and Mount Brooks are all within a one-day paddle or skiff trip from Brooks Camp and are excellent day hikes. Park rangers and lodge employees can provide additional information on routes and attractions.

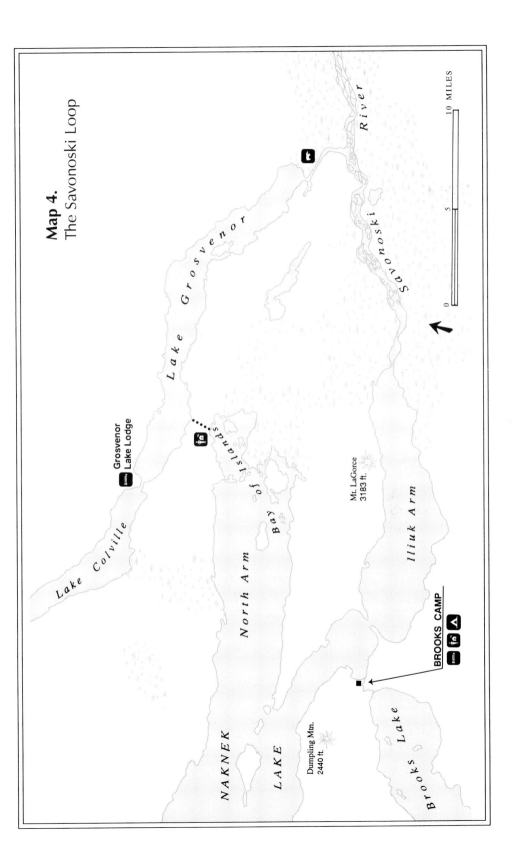

Map 4.
The Savonoski Loop

Lake Colville

Lake Grosvenor

Grosvenor
Lake Lodge

Savonoski

River

Islands

of

Bay

North Arm

Mt. LaGorce
3183 ft.

Iliuk Arm

NAKNEK

LAKE

Dumpling Mtn.
2440 ft.

BROOKS CAMP

Brooks

Lake

0   5   10 MILES

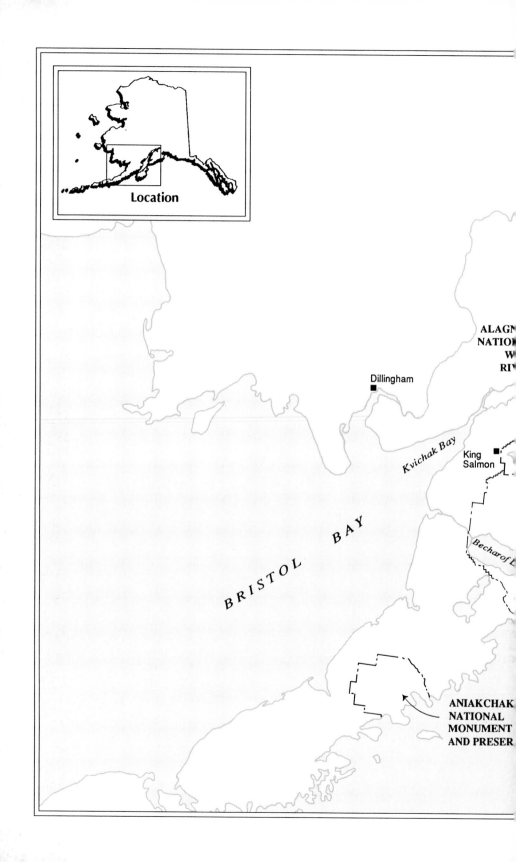

Location

ALAGN
NATIO
W
RIV

Dillingham

Kvichak Bay

King
Salmon

BRISTOL   BAY

Becharof L

ANIAKCHAK
NATIONAL
MONUMENT
AND PRESER

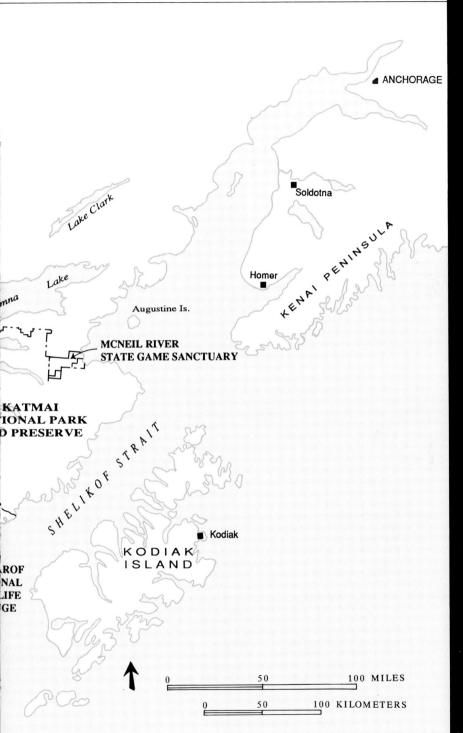

ANCHORAGE

Lake Clark

Soldotna

mna Lake

Augustine Is.

Homer

KENAI PENINSULA

MCNEIL RIVER
STATE GAME SANCTUARY

KATMAI
IONAL PARK
D PRESERVE

SHELIKOF STRAIT

Kodiak

KODIAK
ISLAND

AROF
NAL
IFE
GE

0   50   100 MILES

0   50   100 KILOMETERS

Ukinrek Maars. U. S. FISH AND WILDLIFE SERVICE

Becharof at a glance

Size: 1,200,000 acres
(486 hectares)
Elevations: 0 to 4800 feet
(0 to 1470 meters)
Established: 1978
Access via: King Salmon
Primary recreation: wildlife
viewing, wilderness, fishing
Best time to visit: June to
September

USGS maps (1:250,000):
Karluk, Mt. Katmai, Naknek,
Ugashik
For further information:
Refuge Manager
Becharof National
Wildlife Refuge
P.O. Box 277
King Salmon, AK 99613
(907) 246-3339

CHAPTER 15

Becharof National Wildlife Refuge

Becharof National Wildlife Refuge is named for 450-square-mile Becharof Lake, the second largest lake in Alaska. The refuge is home to brown bear, moose, caribou, and waterfowl, and is the spawning ground for almost a million sockeye salmon each year. Above the glittering lakes and wetlands where swans, ducks, and other waterfowl nest, the snowy spires of Mount Peulik and the Kejulik Pinnacles rise toward the sky.

Before the *Exxon Valdez* oil spill, Puale Bay on the outer coast of Becharof was famous for its thriving seabird colonies, among the largest on the Alaska Peninsula. Murres, puffins, kittiwakes, and cormorants nested on the rocky bluffs. Below them, harbor seals and sea lions hauled out on the rocky shores, up to 5,000 at one time.

In 1989, Puale Bay was smeared with crude oil spilled from the supertanker *Exxon Valdez* nearly 400 miles away. According to the Alaska Department of Environmental Conservation, Puale Bay was one of the most heavily-oiled locations outside of Prince William Sound. Common and thick-billed murres were especially affected by the oil spill and may have altered their nesting behavior as a result. U.S. Fish and Wildlife Service staff observed an oiled brown bear in Puale Bay in 1989. Studies to assess impacts in Puale Bay and elsewhere continue as of this writing.

When Congress established Becharof National Wildlife Refuge in 1980, it also set aside three other refuges on the Alaska Peninsula: the Alaska Peninsula NWR, the Alaska Peninsula unit of the Alaska

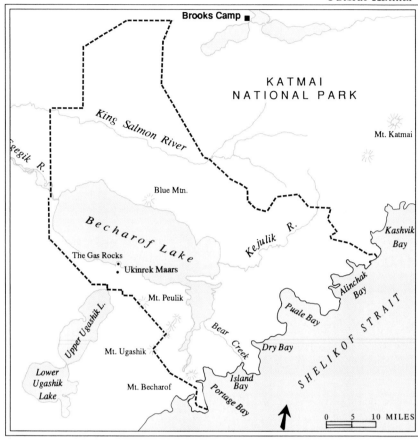

Map 6. Becharof National Wildlife Refuge

Mt. Peulik. U. S. FISH AND WILDLIFE SERVICE

Maritime Refuge, and the Izembek Refuge. Together, these four refuges comprise an area the size of New Jersey.

These public lands are used for subsistence hunting and fishing by Natives and other local residents. Hunters come seeking caribou, moose and brown bear, while anglers find salmon, rainbow trout, arctic char, grayling and lake trout.

A portage route through Becharof was favored by Russians and Natives during the 1800s and the settlement of Kanatak grew up on the coast. Several exploratory oil wells were drilled in Becharof in the 1930s, at which time Kanatak grew from a population of 23 to 134. Exploration results were not promising to the oil industry and the town soon shrunk to its earlier size. Kanatak was abandoned in 1981 when fire destroyed the Russian Orthodox church and most of the village.

Strange Volcanos

The **Ukinrek Maars**, two huge steam explosion craters, formed in a series of eruptions from March 30 through April 9, 1977. Magma rising from deep in the earth encountered groundwater, which vaporized instantly. The expanding steam blasted through the surface of the earth along major fractures related to underlying tectonic plate margins. The explosions sent steam and ash clouds three miles (six km) into the sky and dusted the land with ash for a distance of 100 miles (160 km). Native school-children who visited the craters, or maars, shortly after the eruption first called them *Ukinrek*, which means "two holes in the ground" in the Yup'ik language.

The maars are located on the south side of Becharof Lake on the Bruin Bay Fault, a regional geologic feature that is discussed in Chapter 3. Geologists believe that the fault intersects a tectonic boundary at this location. The resulting fractures provided conduits for the rising magma.

Gas Rocks, another volcanic feature in Becharof, is an outcrop of fractured rock on the Bruin Bay Fault where carbon dioxide gas is constantly emitted. It is linked to the same fracture system as the Ukinrek Maars.

Mount Peulik, which means "one with smoke" in Yup'ik, is not connected hydraulically with the Maars and Gas Rocks magma system. Mount Peulik erupted in 1814 and in 1852.

Aniakchak caldera.   NATIONAL PARK SERVICE

Aniakchak at a glance

Size: 586,000 acres
(237 000 hectares)
Elevations: 0 to 4400 feet
(0 to 1300 meters)
Established: 1978
Primary attractions: volcanic
features, wilderness, rafting
Aniakchak River
Access via: King Salmon
Best time to visit: June to
September

USGS maps (1:250,000):
Bristol Bay, Chignik, Sutwik
Island, Ugashik
For further information:
Aniakchak National Monument
and Preserve
National Park Service
P.O. Box 7
King Salmon, Alaska 99613
(907) 246-3305

CHAPTER 16

Aniakchak National Monument and Preserve

Aniakchak National Monument and Preserve is a wild and rugged treasure set aside by Congress in 1980. Located at the base of the Alaska Peninsula some 400 miles (640 kilometers) southwest of Anchorage, Aniakchak is reached only by charter aircraft or boat.

The intrepid visitor to Aniakchak will find some of the world's most recent and unique volcanic features, the Aniakchak Wild River that drops through class IV whitewater to the Pacific, and some of the harshest weather on the continent. One of the least-visited areas in the entire National Park System, Aniakchak has no visitor facilities, no campgrounds, indeed, no roads.

The weather in Aniakchak has a fearsome temperament and travel delays are almost a certainty. Summer temperatures average in the 40s and 50s (degrees Fahrenheit) and most days are overcast and wet. The caldera creates its own weather with violent wind and rainstorms funneling through the Gates. Many visitors to the caldera are dropped off on Surprise Lake. Other access points include Meshik Lake, or Aniakchak, Amber or Kujulik Bays on the Pacific Ocean. Air taxis can be chartered from King Salmon, Port Heiden, or possibly other towns.

Subsistence users and sportsmen hunt and fish in Aniakchak, while commercial fishermen are the primary users of Aniakchak National Preserve coastline. Experienced whitewater boaters paddle the Aniakchak River, and geologists and other adventurers visit the caldera. The monument is contained on the Chignik and Sutwik Island section (1:250,000) maps.

Aniakchak is two bays away from the fishing community of Chignik. Much of its rich history is linked to fishing and shares themes common with the rest of the Alaska Peninsula. There is enough material to fill a book about Aniakchak; the information presented in this chapter is just an introduction to this remote national monument and preserve.

The National Park Service maintains a ranger station in Aniakchak Bay, a renovated Alaska Packers Association cabin that is sometimes staffed by park rangers.

Aniakchak Caldera

Suddenly the rim fell from below us, and there we were flying over the world's largest crater while it was in active eruption.

The awfulness of the sight stunned me. It was the most terrible prelude of hell I could ever imagine. Last year it was a plant, fish, and animal world inside of a mountain where colour and variety abounded, in the thirty-square-mile area closed in by 3000-foot walls. Now it was the abomination of desolation with everything blotted out. ...Caught in a down draught, the plane turned over, pointing its nose straight down as we were sucked toward the erupting mass of hot gases. There was only one way to regain our air speed, and Blunt, with admirable presence of mind, was equal to the emergency! He dived the plane straight down, and with the speed of the dive righted the plane and roared away back into the Aniakchak Canyon through a huge rift in the volcano walls.

Father Bernard Hubbard
Explorer and Jesuit priest [1]

Father Hubbard was on a steamer enroute to Aniakchak Caldera in 1931 when it began shooting clouds of ash and pumice into the sky. Hubbard's explorations of the astonishing caldera the previous summer had prompted him to return for another season. He convinced daredevil bush pilot Harry Blunt and co-pilot Al Munson to fly into the erupting volcano with Hubbard as a passenger.

Hubbard and his geology students returned a month

---

[1] Reprinted with the permission of The America Press from *Mush, You Malemutes!*, by Bernard R. Hubbard, ©1932, pp. 52-53.

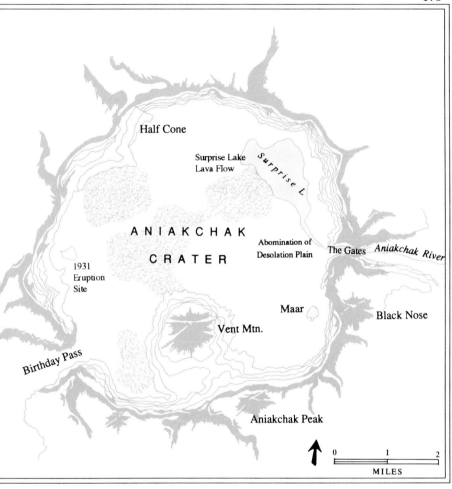

Map 7. Aniakchak Caldera

after the eruption ceased to investigate this "valley of death." They compared it with the lush green world of the previous summer where they had observed numerous orchids, rambling brown bears, and caribou. Hubbard was ecstatic about the eruption because he had asserted that the caldera was still active, contrary to the pronouncement by the U.S. Geological Survey that it was not. Not until 1922 had the Survey discovered the enormous caldera that was hidden behind clouds in the center of the Alaska Peninsula.

Ashes from the May, 1931 eruption of Aniakchak fell at the rate of a pound an hour in Chignik, 65 miles (100 kilometers) to the south. The blast was heard 200 miles (320 kilometers) away and the ash sprinkled the ground nearly 700 miles (1,100 kilometers) from the source. The ash flows from the eruption traveled up and over topographic barriers several hundred feet high and covered a 1,000 square-mile area. In spite of the scale of the eruption — one of the world's largest during recent times — the eruption center of the 1931 event is just one small vent inside the enormous Aniakchak Caldera. Six miles

(10 kilometers) across and 3,000 feet (1000 meters) deep, the caldera formed 3,500 years ago with the eruption and ensuing collapse of a 7,000-foot mountain.

Relics of Aniakchak's volcanic past — cinder cones, lava flows, caldera lakes, maars and pumice deposits — scatter the floor of the immense caldera. One could spend days exploring these volcanic features in the company of the plants and animals that have returned to the caldera.

Vent Mountain looms 2,200 feet (670 meters) above the floor of the caldera, a prominent volcano within the volcano. Several lava flows radiate down the slopes of Vent Mountain. One flow stretches to Surprise Lake, a milky turquoise lake 2.5 miles long in the northeast portion of the caldera. Tongues of the half-mile-wide lava flow form cliffs a hundred feet high above Surprise Lake, defining a series of coves on the southwest shore of the lake.

Lake terrace deposits ring the shoreline above the current water level, indicating that the lake once filled 50 per cent or more of the caldera. It eventually breached the caldera rim and carved through the wall of the volcano to form the Gates, the outlet of the wild Aniakchak River.

The Black Nose, a great obsidian cliff, guards the south side of the Gates; fossil-bearing sedimentary rocks are found on the lower portions of the Gates. The 1931 eruption burst over the western wall of the caldera halfway between Birthday Pass and Half Cone. It left a crater one-half mile across and nearly 250 feet (75 meters) deep with a small lava dome in the bottom.

Aniakchak River

For boaters, the Aniakchak River is a challenging river that tumbles from the crater lake of an active volcano to the Pacific Ocean. It originates in Surprise Lake and carves through the Gates, the crater edge which rises more than a thousand feet on each side of the river. The river surges through Class IV whitewater as it drops more than 1,000 feet in the first 15 miles of its 27-mile course. The final 12 miles is a mellow, meandering float through open tundra. Boaters may want to dayhike along the route or from the lagoon at the end. Brown bears are common in the area.

The usual hazards of run-ning a wild river are amplified on the Aniakchak by the extreme isolation, cold water and harsh weather conditions. Equipment recommendations include extra rope for lining boats, extensive patching materials (including speedy stitcher), spare paddles and life vests, and proper personal gear for a challenging float trip in potentially bad weather. Only a few parties attempt the river each year.

The Route

The first mile out of Surprise Lake is the smooth and easy lull before the storm. Once the river reaches the Gates, boaters had better be prepared for a Class III and IV fast and rocky dodge through narrow canyons and shallow water. Boaters should definitely scout the Gates before attempting to run it. The south side is better for portaging and lining.

After the Gates, the river basin widens but the river stays rocky and shallow in Class II whitewater. At about mile 6 (section 13), the river narrows into a gorge with a vertical wall on the north side followed by a chute where the water is deep and powerful, estimated as Class III. Boaters should be extra cautious through this area. As the river approaches Hidden Creek, in sections 19, 20, and 29, it becomes deeper and less rocky, lapsing into Class II. Hidden Creek emerges with a fury, and as one rafter described:

We never did see where Hidden Creek entered the Aniakchak, but we sure experienced it. We began by maneuvering through a 10-foot gap between two car-sized rocks and then immediately shot over and down a two- to four-foot falls. After avoiding another large rock, the river abruptly turned 180º to the left, requiring us to do some serious and powerful back paddling to avoid slamming into a 25-foot vertical rock wall. What made these obstacles exciting was that they probably only occurred within a 50 yard stretch of the river. Jack [Mosby] rated the whitewater at Hidden Creek as Class III.

David Manski

The valley opens up below Hidden Creek, providing a view of Pinnacle Mountain. The river braids out for about a mile and a half before converging on itself into a meandering Class I river beyond Pinnacle Mountain. The last eight- to ten miles are a relaxing float where bald eagles, tundra swans, and ducks may be spotted. The outlet at Aniakchak Lagoon is shallow, so it may be advisable to avoid the area at low tide.

River runners note: the river classes given above can vary significantly; water conditions can change daily due to storms.

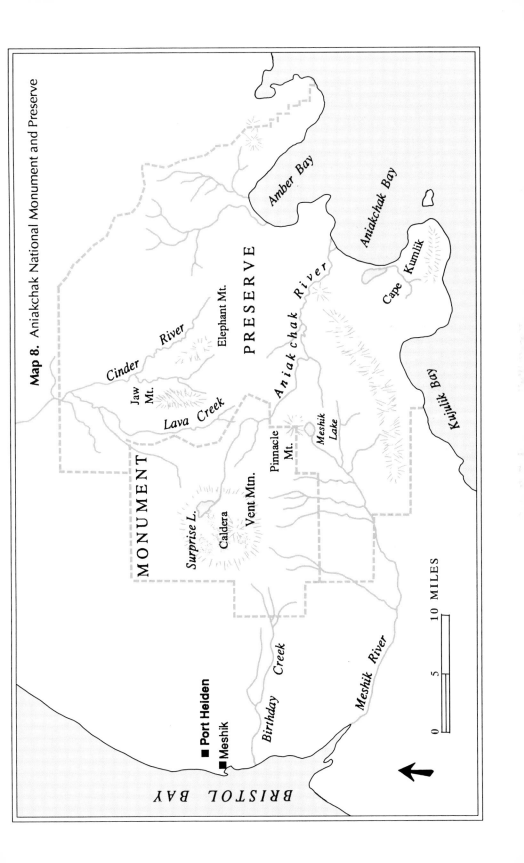

Map 8. Aniakchak National Monument and Preserve

■ **Bears at McNeil River falls.** LEO KEELER

McNeil at a glance

Size: 85,000 acres (34 000 hectares)
Elevations: 0 to 4700 ft.
(0 to 1400 m)
Established: 1967
Access via: Homer
Best visited: May-October
Primary recreation: photographing
wild bears, fishing
USGS maps (1:63,360):
 Iliamna A-4

*Information and permit
applications are available
from:*

Alaska Department of Fish and
Game
Wildlife Conservation Division
333 Raspberry Road
Anchorage, Alaska 99518
(907) 344-0541

CHAPTER 17

McNeil River State Game Sanctuary

McNeil River State Game Sanctuary adjoins Katmai National Park and Preserve to the north. Many of the same conditions that make Katmai such prime bear habitat are found at McNeil River as well. In fact, McNeil Falls attracts even more bears than does Brooks Falls in Katmai. McNeil is famous for the large brown bear population and for the opportunity it affords for watching bears fishing and interacting in a natural setting.

Permits

Permit Lottery

The Alaska Department of Fish and Game (ADF&G) manages the McNeil River State Game Sanctuary, stating its primary intent as the protection of brown bears. To limit the number of visitors to McNeil, ADF&G awards permits by means of a lottery. It allows only ten people to watch bears at the falls each day from July 1 through August 25.

Permits may be available for dates before July 1, but these are not pre-issued by lottery. In June, sockeye salmon attract bears to Mikfik Creek, which drains into McNeil Cove.

Each permit is issued for a four-day block of time; applicants specify first and second choices for dates on their application. A computer randomly chooses permit winner names approximately April 15. Winners are notified by mail a few weeks later

In 1990, fewer than one in ten applicants received permits. The deadline for filing applications is April 1. A $50 fee ($40 of which is refunded within 60-90 days to unsuccessful applicants) for each name listed on the application was required in 1991 with the permit application.

Standby Permits

In addition to the regular bear-viewing permits, the Department of Fish and Game issues standby permits. A standby permit allows people to fill unused bear viewing slots of those permit holders who choose not to visit the falls on all four of their permitted days. A standby permit entitles a person to stay in the McNeil campground for a limited time waiting for such an opening to occur. If a slot opens up, it is filled with standby visitors on a first-come, first-served basis. A standby permit does not guarantee the opportunity to view bears.

Standby permittees are charged a use fee upon their arrival in the sanctuary. Standby permits are available only from the Homer office, by phone or in person. Contact ADF&G [(907) 235-8191] for more information.

Getting to McNeil

Visitors must fly to McNeil by air taxi, usually from King Salmon or Homer. Arrangements should be made well in advance as permit holders must be at the campground no later than 9am on any day they want to use their permit to view bears. Many people prefer to arrive the day before the permit begins.

What to Bring

There are no commercial visitor facilities available at McNeil so visitors must come prepared to camp out and cook their own food. Hip waders are essential for crossing the creeks and McNeil Lagoon to reach the falls. Visitors should bring a sturdy tent, sleeping bag and pad, a cookstove, flashlight, quality raingear, warm clothing, mosquito repellant, headnet and enough food to last several days longer than their intended stay.

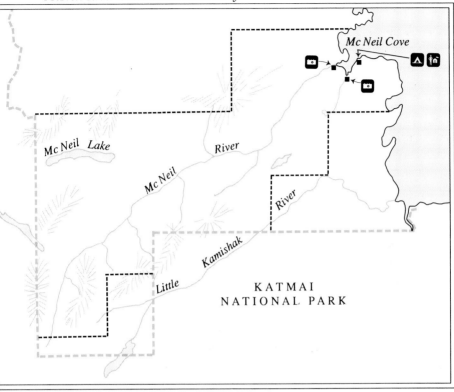

Map 9. McNeil River State Game Sanctuary

■ **Alagnak National Wild River.** JEAN BODEAU

Alagnak River at a glance

Trip lengths: 66 to 74 miles
(105 to 115 km)
Elevations: 0 to 800 feet
Established: 1980
Access via: King Salmon
Primary recreation: fishing,
wilderness, floating, wildlife
Best time to visit: June to
September
USGS maps (1:63,360):
Iliamna A-7, A-8;
Dillingham A-1, A-2, A-3

For further information:
Alagnak National Wild River
c/o Katmai National Park and
Preserve
P.O. Box 7
King Salmon, AK 99613
(907) 246-3305

CHAPTER 18

Alagnak National Wild River

The Alagnak River adjoins Katmai National Park and Preserve and is a popular trip for rafters and anglers wishing to fish in a wilderness setting.

The Upper Alagnak River, and the Nonvianuk River which joins it in the upper reaches, are known for their wild rainbow trout stocks. Dolly Varden, grayling, and sockeye salmon are among the other species that anglers find in abundance in the Alagnak River.

The Alagnak tumbles from Kukaklek Lake down to its confluence with the Nonvianuk River. From there, it fans across the tundra in lazy braids to the Kvichak River which forms the uppermost tip of Bristol Bay. Osprey and eagles soar over the Alagnak, and beaver lodges dot the shores. Brown bears pace the banks of the river, especially when the salmon are running.

The Alagnak was designated as a National Wild River in 1980 with the passage of ANILCA.

The Route

Boaters have their choice of two variations for trips on the river. The Nonvianuk River variation is shorter (11 miles to confluence) and easier with Class I whitewater. This option begins at the outlet of Nonvianuk Lake. The water verges on Class II in places, particularly above the confluence. Rafts, kayaks or canoes could navigate the Nonvianuk River.

The Upper Alagnak from Kukaklek Lake is a longer (19

miles to confluence) and more difficult option with a set of Class III rapids in a steep canyon before the confluence with the Nonvianuk River. These rapids are located about two-thirds of the way down the upper portion of the river immediately after the river makes a 90-degree bend. The steep rock walls of the canyon make portaging around the rapids difficult. Those who consider boating the Upper Alagnak River should have lots of whitewater experience.

Water levels are usually lower in May and June than they are in mid- to-late summer. Boaters intending to float the Upper Alagnak should be experienced and have a sturdy raft. Canoes are not appropriate for the Upper Alagnak River and kayakers attempting the river should be experienced whitewater boaters and accomplished at performing Eskimo rolls.

The total length of the Nonvianuk River variation is approximately 66 miles, while the total length of the Upper Alagnak variation is roughly 74 miles. The trips can take anywhere from two days to a week, depending on water conditions, the amount of time spent fishing, and the take-out location.

Access and Camping

Boaters will need to charter aircraft to drop them at the starting point of their trip. Charters are available from King Salmon, Iliamna, Soldotna, Homer and Brooks Camp. National Park Service rangers sometimes are posted at the outlet of Nonvianuk Lake on the south side of the river. Boaters should contact the rangers before setting out on the river.

A handful of cabins are maintained on the north side of the river by the park concessionaire. They have been operated intermittently by Battle Lake Wilderness Lodge, which also conducts guided rafting/ fishing trips on the river.

People can camp on either side of the river on Nonvianuk Lake.

The ruins of Knox "Bill" Hammersley's cabin stand on the north side of the river. Hammersley was a trapper who lived alone for many years in the cabin.

Land on both sides of Kukaklek Lake at the outlet of the Upper Alagnak River are owned by Native corporations.

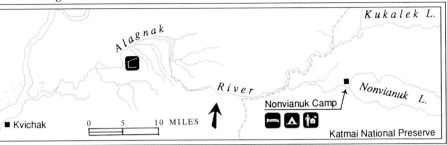

Map 10. Alagnak National Wild River

There is a one-acre campsite easement for boaters on the north side of the river, atop the bluff.

Native allotments and occasional cabins dot the lower portions of the Alagnak River. When choosing camping sites here, boaters and anglers should be aware that some of the land is private. Campers are encouraged to use existing campsites (as long as they are clean) when they find them in order to concentrate impacts. Brown bears are common, particularly during the salmon runs, so campers should take precautions to prevent bear encounters. Giardiasis is found in Alagnak River water, so boil your drinking water for at least five minutes, treat it with iodine or filter it.

Most people end their float trip at least ten miles upstream of the confluence with the Kvichak River. Below this point the river is sluggish and much of the land is privately owned.

One take-out is just beyond McCormick's cabin, a corrugated metal cabin on the south side of the river. There are several tent sites and a fire ring here but since this spot is private land, you should not camp here.

McCormick's is approximately a one-hour float beyond Agnes Estrada's rustic log cabin (you may see caribou antlers hung above the door). She lived in the cabin for most of her life, snaring animals until she was nearly 90 years old.

The old townsite of Levelock, located just below McCormick's cabin, was abandoned when the villagers moved downstream to the current village of Levelock. An hour float beyond McCormick's is Katmai Lodge, a fishing lodge with a runway and a floatplane dock.

Agness Estrada cabin, a landmark along the Alagnak.
ANTONIA FOWLER

Lodges on the Alagnak

Katmai Lodge is a fishing lodge located on the lower portion of the Alagnak River known for its guided fishing trips with jet boat. The lodge has indoor plumbing and heated rooms for up to 80 guests. Meals are served in a central dining area. Other amenities include a lounge and sauna. The lodge has a runway for wheeled aircraft as well as a floatplane dock. For further information contact:

Katmai Lodge
Tony Sarp
2825 90th S.E.
Everett, WA 98208
(206) 337-0326

The Conways guide rafting/fishing trips on the Alagnak River. These trips can be arranged alone or in conjunction with a stay at the primitive cabins at Battle Lake in the northern part of Katmai National Park. For further information contact:

Tim and Wendy Conway
8076 Caribbean Way
Sacramento, CA 95826
(916) 381-0250
(907) 243-5448

Located about four miles upstream of the confluence with the Kvichak River, the Alagnak Lodge is a fly-in wilderness fishing lodge that specializes in salmon and rainbow trout fishing. The lodge accommodates up to 21 guests at a time. For further information contact:

Dick Roccanova
Route 2, Box 275
Cheney, WA 99004
(509) 456-8722

Other lodges include:

Branch River Lodge
10210 N. E. 189th St.
Bothell, WA 98011
(206) 487-2077

Royal Wolf Lodge
P. O. Box 191007
Anchorage, AK 99519
(907) 248-3256

Appendix

APPENDIX

Bird, Mammal and Wildflower Checklists

Bird Checklist

Loons, Grebes, Shearwaters, Storm
Petrels and Cormorants

___ Common loon
___ Pacific loon
___ Red-throated loon
___ Red-necked grebe
___ Horned grebe
___ Fork-tailed storm-petrel
___ Sooty shearwater
___ Double-crested cormorant

Ducks, Geese and Swans

___ Tundra swan
___ Canada goose
___ Brant
___ Greater white-fronted goose
___ Mallard
___ Northern pintail
___ American widgeon
___ Northern shoveler
___ Gadwall
___ Green-winged teal
___ Blue-winged teal
___ Greater scaup
___ Common goldeneye
___ Barrow's goldeneye
___ Bufflehead
___ Harlequin duck
___ Ruddy duck
___ Common eider
___ King eider
___ Spectacled eider

___ Steller's eider
___ Oldsquaw
___ Black scoter
___ White-winged scoter
___ Surf scoter
___ Common merganser
___ Hooded merganser
___ Red-breasted merganser

Accipiters and Falcons

___ Northern goshawk
___ Northern harrier
___ Rough-legged hawk
___ Golden eagle
___ Bald eagle
___ Osprey
___ Gyrfalcon
___ Peregrine falcon
___ Merlin
___ American kestrel

Grouse and Ptarmigan

___ Spruce grouse
___ Willow ptarmigan
___ Rock ptarmigan

Cranes, Oystercatchers, Plovers and Sandpipers

___ Sandhill crane
___ Black oystercatcher
___ Lesser golden plover
___ Black-bellied plover
___ Semipalmated plover
___ Whimbrel
___ Solitary sandpiper
___ Spotted sandpiper
___ Rock sandpiper
___ Pectoral sandpiper
___ Baird's sandpiper
___ Least sandpiper
___ Western sandpiper
___ Wandering tattler
___ Greater yellowlegs
___ Lesser yellowlegs
___ Short-billed dowitcher
___ Long-billed dowitcher
___ Surfbird
___ Ruddy turnstone
___ Dunlin
___ Marbled godwit
___ Red phalarope
___ Red-necked phalarope
___ Common snipe
___ Black turnstone

Jaegers, Gulls and Terns

___ Parasitic jaeger
___ Long-tailed jaeger
___ Glaucous-winged gull
___ Herring gull
___ Mew gull
___ Bonaparte's gull
___ Slaty-backed gull
___ Black-legged kittiwake
___ Arctic tern
___ Aleutian tern

Alcids

___ Common murre
___ Marbled murrelet
___ Pigeon guillemot

___ Horned puffin
___ Tufted puffin
___ Kittlitz murrelet

Owls

___ Great horned owl
___ Short-eared owl
___ Snowy owl
___ Boreal owl
___ Northern hawk-owl

Hummingbirds, Kingfishers, Woodpeckers and Flycatchers

___ Rufous hummingbird
___ Belted kingfisher
___ Downy woodpecker
___ Three-toed woodpecker
___ Alder flycatcher
___ Olive-sided flycatcher
___ Say's phoebe

Larks and Swallows

___ Horned lark
___ Cliff swallow
___ Violet-green swallow
___ Bank swallow
___ Tree swallow

Jays, Magpies, Crows and Shrikes

___ Gray jay
___ Black-billed magpie
___ Common raven
___ Northwestern crow
___ Northern shrike

Chickadees, Nuthatches, Dippers and Creepers

___ Black-capped chickadee
___ Boreal chickadee
___ Dipper
___ Red-breasted nuthatch
___ Brown creeper

Blackbirds, Tanagers, Sparrows and Buntings

___ Rusty blackbird
___ Pine grosbeak
___ Rosy finch
___ Common redpoll
___ Hoary redpoll
___ White-winged crossbill
___ Red crossbill
___ Dark-eyed junco
___ Savannah sparrow
___ American tree sparrow
___ Golden-crowned sparrow
___ White-crowned sparrow
___ Fox sparrow
___ Song sparrow
___ Lapland longspur
___ Snow bunting

Kinglets, Thrushes, Pipits and Warblers

___ Golden-crowned kinglet
___ Ruby-crowned kinglet
___ American robin
___ Varied thrush
___ Gray-cheeked thrush
___ American pipit
___ Arctic warbler
___ Orange-crowned warbler
___ Yellow warbler
___ Yellow-rumped warbler
___ Blackpoll warbler
___ Wilson's warbler
___ Northern waterthrush
___ Swainson's thrush
___ Hermit thrush

Mammal Checklist

Insectivores

___ Arctic or tundra shrew   *Sorex arcticus*
___ Common or masked shrew   *Sorex cinereus*
___ Dusky or vagrant shrew   *Sorex vagrans*
___ Little brown bat   *Myotis lucifugus*

Hares

___ Snowshoe or varying hare   *Lepus americanus*
___ Arctic or tundra hare   *Lepus timidus*

Rodents

___ Arctic ground squirrel   *Citelus parryii*
___ Beaver   *Castor canadensis*
___ Hoary marmot   *Marmota caligata*
___ Meadow jumping mouse   *Zapus hudsonius*
___ Meadow vole   *Microtus pennsylvanicus*
___ Muskrat   *Ondotra zibethica*
___ Northern bog lemming (mouse)   *Synaptomys borealis*
___ Northern red backed mouse or vole *Clethrionomys rutilus*

___ Porcupine   *Erethizon dorsatum*
___ Red squirrel   *Tamiasciurus hudsonicus*
___ Tundra vole   *Microtus oeconomus*

Wolves and foxes

___ Red fox   *Vulpes sp.*
___ Wolf   *Canis lupus*

Bears

___ Brown bear   *Ursus arctos*

Ungulates

___ Barren ground caribou   *Rangifer tarandus*
___ Moose   *Alces sp.*

Weasels and Allies

___ Ermine (short-tailed weasel)   *Mustela erminea*
___ River otter   *Lutra canadensis*
___ Mink   *Mustela vison*
___ Least weasel   *Mustela rixosa*
___ Wolverine   *Gulo sp.*

Cats

___ Lynx   *Lynx canadensis*

Marine Mammals

___ Harbor or Pacific hair seal   *Phoca vitulina*
___ Beluga whale   *Delphinapterus leucas*
___ Sea otter   *Enhydra lutris*
___ Steller sea lion   *Eumetopias jubata*

Wildflower and Herb Checklist

Bluebell Family

___ Mountain harebell/Bluebell   *Campanula lasiocarpa*
___ Bluebells of Scotland   *Campanula rotundifolia*

Buckwheat Family

___ Mountain sorrel   *Oxyria digyna*
___ Alpine meadow bistort   *Polygonum viviparum*
___ Arctic dock   *Rumex arcticus*

Composite Family

___ Yarrow   *Achillea borealis*
___ Pussytoes   *Antennaria sp.*
___ Arnica   *Arnica sp.*
___ Frigid arnica   *Arnica frigida*
___ Common wormwood   *Artemisia Tilesii*
___ Siberian aster   *Aster sibiricus*
___ Arctic daisy   *Chrysanthemum arcticum*
___ Fleabane   *Erigeron peregrinus*
___ Coltsfoot   *Petasites sp.*
___ Rattlesnake root   *Prenanthes alata*
___ Ragworts, Fleabanes   *Senecio sp.*
___ Goldenrod   *Solidago sp.*

Crowfoot Family

___ Monkshood   *Aconitum delphinifolium*
___ Baneberry   *Actaea rubra*
___ Narcissus-flowered anemone   *Anemone narcissiflora*
___ Marsh marigold   *Caltha palustris*
___ Larkspur   *Delphinium glaucum*
___ Buttercup   *Ranunculus sp.*

Evening Primrose

___ Fireweed   *Epilobium angustifolium*
___ River beauty/Dwarf fireweed   *Epilobium latifolium*
___ Willow herb   *Epilobium sp.*

Figwort Family

___ Indian paintbrush   *Castilleja sp.*
___ Lagotis/Weasel Snout   *Lagotis glauca*
___ Yellow monkey flower   *Mimulus guttatus*
___ Lousewort   *Pedicularis sp.*

Gentian Family

___ Glaucous gentian   *Gentiana glauca*
___ Star gentian   *Swertia perennis*

Heath Family

___ Bog rosemary   *Andromeda polifolia*
___ Alaska cassiope   *Cassiope lycopodioides*
___ Starry cassiope/
     Alaska moss heather   *Cassiope stelleriana*
___ Alpine azalea   *Loiseleuria procumbens*
___ Mountain heather/
     Aleutian heather   *Phyllodoce aleutica*

Lily Family

___ Wild chive   *Allium schoenoprasum*
___ Chocolate lily   *Fritillaria camschatcensis*
___ Alp lily   *Lloydia serotina*
___ Twisted stalk/Watermelon berry   *Streptopus amplexifolius*

Madder Family

___ Northern bedstraw   *Galium boreale*
___ Sweet-scented bedstraw   *Galium triflorum*

Mustard Family

___ Rock cress   *Arabis sp.*
___ Purple cress/Bitter cress   *Cardamine purpurea*
___ Yellow cress   *Rorippa sp.*

Orchis Family

___ Coral root   *Corallorriza trifida*
___ Key flower/Rose-purple orchis   *Dactylorhiza aristata*
___ Small northern bog orchid   *Platanthera obtusata*
___ Ladies' tresses   *Spiranthes Romanzoffiana*

Parsley Family

___ Water hemlock   *Cicuta Mackenzieana*
___ Cow parsnip   *Heracleum lanatum*

Pea Family

___ Arctic milk vetch   *Astragalus alpinus*
___ Hairy arctic milk vetch   *Astragalus umbellatus*
___ Beach pea   *Lathyrus maritimus*
___ Nootka lupine   *Lupinus nootkatensis*
___ Oxytrope   *Oxytropis maydelliana*
___ Blackish oxytrope   *Oxytropis nigrescens*

Pink Family

___ Mouse ear chickweed   *Cerastrium sp.*
___ Sandwort   *Minuartia macrocarpa*
___ Grove sandwort   *Moehringia lateriflora*
___ Moss campion   *Silene acaulis*

Polemonium Family

___ Tall Jacob's ladder   *Polemonium acutiflorum*
___ Jacob's ladder   *Polemonium pulcherrimum*

Poppy Family

___ Alaska poppy   *Papaver alaskanum*
___ Pink poppy   *Papaver alboroseum*

Primrose Family

___ Shooting star   *Dodecatheon pulchellum*
___ Pixie eyes/Wedge leaved primrose   *Primula cunifolia*
___ Chukchi primrose   *Primula tschuktschorum*
___ Starflower   *Trientalis europaea*

Rose Family

___ Mountain avens   *Dryas sp.*
___ Avens   *Geum sp.*
___ Luetkea/Alaska spirea   *Luetkea pectinata*
___ Silverweed   *Potentilla Egedii*
___ Shrubby cinquefoil/Tundra rose   *Potentilla fruticosa*
___ Marsh fivefinger   *Potentilla palustris*
___ Villous cinquefoil   *Potentilla uniflora*
___ Prickly wild rose   *Rosa acicularis*
___ Sitka burnet   *Sanguisorba stipulata*

Saxifrage Family

___ Alpine heuchera   *Heuchera glabra*
___ Bog star/Grass-of-parnassus   *Parnassia palustris*

___ Spotted saxifrage   *Saxifraga bronchialis*
___ Cushion saxifrage   *Saxifraga Eschscholtzii*
___ Spider plant   *Saxifraga flagellaris*
___ Bog saxifrage/
     Yellow marsh saxifrage   *Saxifraga hirculus*
___ Snow saxifrage   *Saxifraga nivalis*
___ Brook saxifrage/
     Heart-leaved saxifrage   *Saxifraga punctata*

Violet Family

___ Stream violet/Yellow violet   *Viola glabella*
___ Alaska violet   *Viola Langsdorffii*

Wintergreen Family

___ Single delight   *Moneses uniflora*
___ Pink pyrola/Wintergreen   *Pyrola asarifolia*

Other Families

___ Broomrape   *Boschniakia rossica*
___ Spring beauty   *Claytonia Chamissoi*
___ Swedish dwarf dogwood   *Cornus suecica*
___ Few-flowered corydalis   *Corydalis pauciflora*
___ Lapland diapensia   *Diapensia lapponicum*
___ Horsetail   *Equisetum sp.*
___ Cotton grass   *Eriophorum sp.*
___ Wild Geranium   *Geranium erianthum*
___ Wild iris/Wild flag   *Iris setosa*
___ Forget-me-not   *Myosotis alpestris*
___ Roseroot/Stonecrop   *Sedum rosea*
___ Valerian   *Valeriana capitata*

Ferns

___ Lady fern   *Athyrium filix-femina*
___ Parsley fern   *Cryptogramma crispa*
___ Fragile fern   *Cystopteris fragilis*
___ Wood fern   *Dryopteris dilatata*
                                        Gymnocarpium dryopteris
                                        Woodsia ilvensis

Club Moss

___ Alpine club moss   *Lycopodium alpinum*
___ Stiff club moss   *Lycopodium annotinum*
___ Common club moss   *Lycopodium clavatum*
___ Fir club moss   *Lycopodium selago*

References and Bibliography

1. General

Alaska Geographic Society, 1989. Katmai Country, Alaska Geographic Vol. 16, No. 1: 95 pg.

Bohn, Dave, 1979. Rambles Through an Alaskan Wild: Katmai and the Valley of the Smokes, Capra Press, Santa Barbara, CA: 175 pg.

Brooks, Alfred Hulse, 1953. Blazing Alaska's Trails, University of Alaska and the Arctic Institute of North America: 528 pg.

Hussey, John A., 1971. Embattled Katmai, A History of Katmai National Monument, National Park Service, Office of History and Historic Architecture, San Francisco: 457 pg.

National Park Service, 1986. General Management Plan, Land Protection Plan, Wilderness Suitability Review, Katmai National Park and Preserve, Alaska.

National Park Service Katmai National Park and Preserve Map, 1990. GPO - 1990—262-100/20006.

National Park Service, 1990-1991. "The Bear Facts: Information About Katmai National Park & Preserve" park newspaper.

National Park Service, 1991. "Brooks River Area Development Concept Plan, Alternatives Workbook, Summer 1991," Katmai National Park and Preserve.

2. A Tale of Red Salmon and Brown Bear

Alaska Quarterly Review, 1986. Alaska Native Writers, Storytellers and Orators, College of Arts and Sciences, University of Alaska Anchorage: 208 pg.

Bledsoe, Thomas, 1987. Brown Bear Summer, Truman Talley Books/ E.P. Dutton, New York: 250 pg.

Childerhouse, R.J. and Marj Trim, 1979. Pacific Salmon, University of Washington Press: 158 pg.

Egbert, Allan L. and Allen W. Stokes, 1974. "The Social Behaviour of Brown Bears on an Alaska Salmon Stream," Third International Conference on Bear Research and Management, No. 40, June, 1974, New York and Moscow: pp. 41-56.

Herrero, Stephen, 1985. Bear Attacks, Their Causes and Avoidance, Lyons & Burford, Publishers, New York: 290 pg.

Morrow, James E., 1980. The Freshwater Fishes of Alaska, Alaska Northwest Publishing Company, Anchorage: 248 pg.

Olson, Tamara L., Barrie K. Gilbert, and Scott H. Fitkin, 1990. "Brown Bear Behavior and Human Activity at Salmon Streams in Katmai National Park, Alaska," Utah State University for National Park Service, Interagency Agreement IA 9700-7-8028: 122 pg.

Shepard, Paul and Barry Sanders, 1985. The Sacred Paw, The Bear in Nature, Myth, and Literature, Viking Penguin Inc.: 244 pg.

Snyder, Gary, 1990. The Practice of the Wild, North Point Press, San Francisco, CA: 190 pg.

3. The Land They Found

Conner, Cathy and Daniel O'Haire, 1988. Roadside Geology of Alaska, Mountain Press Publishing Co., Missoula, MT: pg. 228-232.

Fagan, Brian M., 1987. The Great Journey, The Peopling of Ancient America, Thames and Hudson.

Fisher, Michael A., T.R. Bruns, and R. Von Huene, 1981. "Transverse tectonic boundaries near Kodiak Island, Alaska," GSA Bull. Part I, Vol. 92: pp. 10-18.

Hopkins, David M., 1991. The Bering Land Bridge, for the U.S Postal Stamp commemorating The Bering Land Bridge, first day of issue: Aug. 1991.

Nelson, Edward William, 1899. The Eskimo About Bering Strait, Smithsonian Institution Bureau of American Ethnology, Annual Report 18, 1899: p.482 [Reprinted, Smithsonian Institution Press, 1983.

Reed, B.L. and M.A. Lanphere, 1973. "Plutonic rocks of Alaska-Aleutian Range Batholith," AAPG Memoir 19: pp. 421-428.

Riehle, J.R., E.A. Bailey, S.E. Church, and M.E. Yount, 1989. "Sample locality maps, analytical data, and statistical summary of analyses of rock samples from the Mount Katmai quadrangle and adjacent portions of the Naknek and Afognak quadrangles, Alaska," U.S. Geological Survey Open-File Report 89-570.

Riehle, J.R., and R.L. Detterman, 1988. "Quaternary geologic map of the Mount Katmai quadrangle and adjacent parts of the Naknek and Afognak quadrangles, Alaska", USGS Draft report and map I-2032.

Riehle, J.R., R.L. Detterman, M.E. Yount, and J.W. Miller, 1987. "Preliminary Geologic Map of the Mount Katmai Quadrangle and Portions of the Afognak and Naknek Quadrangles, Alaska," U.S. Geological Survey Open-File Report 87-593, scale 1:250,000.

Sugden, David E. and Brian S. John, 1976. Glaciers and Landscape, Edward Arnold Publishers Ltd.: 376 pg.

4. Beings of the Land

The Alaska-Yukon Wild Flowers Guide, 1974. Alaska Northwest Publishing Company, Anchorage, Alaska: 218 pg.

Cahalane, V.H., 1959. A Biological Survey of Katmai National Monument, Smithsonian Institution Miscellaneous Collections, Washington D.C.: 246 pg.

Calef, George, 1981. Caribou and the Barren Lands, Firefly Books, Ltd., Toronto: 176 pg.

Cooperative Extension Service, University of Alaska Fairbanks and USDA, 1989. Wild Edible and Poisonous Plants of Alaska: 91 pg.

Hoshino, Michio, 1988. Moose, Chronicle Books, San Francisco, CA: 92 pg.

Hultén, Eric, 1968. Flora of Alaska and Neighboring Territories, Stanford University Press, Stanford, California: 1008 pg.

Kari, Priscilla Russell, 1987. Tanaina Plantlore, Dena'ina K'et'una, National Park Service: 205 pg.

Pratt, Verna E., 1989. Alaskan Wildflowers, Alaskakrafts Publishing, Anchorage, Alaska: 136 pg.

Utah State University, Dept. of Fisheries and Wildlife, June 1, 1990. "Brown Bear Behavior and Human Activity at Salmon Streams in Katmai National Park, Alaska", for National Park Service, Alaska Regional Office, Interagency Agreement IA 9700-7-8028: 122 pg.

Viereck, Leslie A. and Elbert L. Little, Jr., 1986. Alaska Trees and Shrubs, University of Alaska Press, Fairbanks, Alaska: 265 pg.

5. The Earliest Inhabitants

Clark, Gerald H., 1977. "Archaeology on the Alaska Peninsula: The Coast of Shelikof Strait 1963-1965," University of Oregon Anthropological Papers No. 13: 247 pg.

Dumond, Don E., 1981. "Archaeology on the Alaska Peninsula: The Naknek Region, 1960-1975," University of Oregon Anthropological Papers No. 21: 277 pg.

Dumond, D.E., 1971. "A Summary of Archaeology in the Katmai Region, Southwestern Alaska," University of Oregon Anthropological Papers No. 2: 61 pg.

Fitzhugh, William W. and Aron Crowell, 1988. Crossroads of Continents, Cultures of Siberia and Alaska, Smithsonian Institute Press: 360 pg.

Harritt, Roger K., 1988. "The Late Prehistory of Brooks River, Alaska: A Model for Analysis of Occupations on the Alaska Peninsula", University of Oregon Anthropological Papers No. 38: 230 pg.

Langdon, Steve J., 1987. The Native People of Alaska, Greatland Graphics, Anchorage: 80 pg.

Mobley, Charles, M., J.C.Haggarty, C.J.Utermohle, M.Eldridge, R.E.Reanier, A.Crowell, B.A.Ream, D.R.Yesner, J.M.Erlandson, and P.E.Buck, 1990. The 1989 EXXON VALDEZ Cultural Resource Program: 300 pg.

6. The Europeans Arrive

Bancroft, Hubert Howe, 1959. History of Alaska 1730 - 1885, Antiquarian Press Ltd. New York: 775 pg.

Hussey, John A., 1971. Embattled Katmai, A History of Katmai National Monument, National Park Service, Office of History and Historic Architecture, San Francisco: 457 pg.

7. Explosion in the Ring of Fire

Eichelberger, John C., 1989. "Direct Observation of a Young Igneous System: A Science Plan for Research Drilling at Katmai, Alaska," submitted to National Park Service (and others): 219 pg.

Eichelberger, J.C., *et al.*, 1990. "Geophysics at Katmai, Geophysical Expedition to Novarupta Volcano, Katmai National Park, Alaska," Eos, Vol. 71, No. 22, May 29, 1990: pp. 733-735.

Fierstein, Judy, 1984. The Valley of Ten Thousand Smokes, Katmai National Park and Preserve, Alaska Natural History Association, Anchorage, AK.

Griggs, Robert F., 1917. "The Valley of Ten Thousand Smokes: National Geographic Society Explorations in the Katmai District of Alaska," National Geographic Magazine: Vol. 31, No. 1, pp. 13-68.

——————, 1918. "The Valley of Ten Thousand Smokes: An Account of the Discovery and Exploration of the Most Wonderful Volcanic Region in the World," National Geographic Magazine: Vol. 33, No. 2, pp. 115-170.

——————, 1919. "The Ten Thousand Smokes Now a National Monument," National Geographic Magazine: Vol. 35, No. 4, pp. 359-366.

——————, 1921. "Our Greatest National Monument," National Geographic Magazine: Vol. 40, No. 3, pp.219-292.

——————, 1922. The Valley of the 10,000 Smokes. National Geographic Society., Washington, D.C.: 341 pg.

Hildreth, Wes, J.E. Fierstein, A. Grunder, and L. Jager, 1981. "The 1912 eruption in the Valley of Ten Thousand Smokes, Katmai National Park: A summary of the stratigraphy and petrology of the ejecta," U.S. Geological Survey Circular 868, The U.S.G.S. in Alaska: Accomplishments During 1981: pp. 37-39.

Hildreth, Wes, 1987. "New perspectives on the eruption of 1912 in the Valley of Ten Thousand Smokes, Katmai National Park, Alaska," Bulletin of Volcanology, Vol. 49, pp. 680-693.

Hubbard, Bernard R., 1932. Mush, You Malemutes!, The America Press, New York: 179 pg.

Hubbard, Bernard R., 1935. Cradle of the Storms, Dodd, Mead and Company, Inc., New York: 285 pg.

Hubbard, Bernard R., 1952. Alaskan Odyssey (British reprint of Mush, You Malemutes!), Robert Hale Ltd., Bristol, England: 198 pg.

Keith, Terry E.C., 1982. "Preliminary observations on fumarole distribution
and alteration, Valley of Ten Thousand Smokes, Alaska," U.S.G.S. Circular
939, The U.S.G.S. in Alaska: Accomplishments During 1982: pp. 82-85.

Martin, George, C., 1912. "Volcanoes of Alaska," National Geographic Magazine: Vol. 23, No. 8, pp. 824-832.

—————, 1913. "The Recent Eruption of Katmai Volcano in Alaska,"
National Geographic Magazine: Vol. 24, No. 2, pp. 131-198.

11. Fishing

Alaska Flyfishers, 1983. Fly Patterns of Alaska, Frank Amato Publications:
88pg.

Rosenbauer, Tom, 1984. The Orvis Fly-Fishing Guide, Nick Lyons Books: 246
pg.

Route, Anthony J., 1989. Flyfishing Alaska, Johnson Publishing Company,
Boulder, CO: 214 pg.

13. The Art of Camping Softly

Hampton, Bruce and David Cole, National Outdoor Leadership School, 1988.
Soft Paths. Stackpole Books: 173 pg.

14. Into the Wilderness

Mosby, Jack and David Dapkus, 1986. Alaska Paddling Guide, J&R Enterprises, Anchorage, AK: 113 pg.

Katmai National Park Service files.

15. Becharof National Wildlife Refuge

Kienle, Juergen, P.R. Kyle, S. Self, R.J. Motyka and V. Lorenz, 1980. "Ukinrek
Maars, Alaska, I. April 1977 Eruption Sequence, Petrology and Tectonic
Setting," Journal of Volcanology and Geothermal Research, Vol. 7: pp. 11-37.

Self, Stephen, J. Kienle, and J.P. Huot, 1980. "Ukinrek Maars, Alaska, II.
Deposits and Formation of the 1977 Craters," Journal of Volcanology and
Geothermal Research, Vol. 7: pp. 39-65.

U.S. Fish and Wildlife Service, 1985. "Becharof National Wildlife Refuge, Final Comprehensive Conservation Plan, Environmental Impact Statement, and Wilderness Review."

U.S. Fish and Wildlife Service map of Alaska Peninsula and Becharof National Wildlife Refuges.

16. Aniakchak National Monument and Preserve

Bosworth, Koren, 1987. "A Vegetation Reconnaissance of Aniakchak Caldera, Alaska," National Park Service report: NPS files, King Salmon, AK.

Miller, Thomas P., and R.L. Smith, 1977. "Spectacular mobility of ash flows around Aniakchak and Fisher calderas, Alaska," Geology, Vol. 5, pp. 173-176.

Mosby, Jack and David Dapkus, 1986. Alaska Paddling Guide, J&R Enterprises, Anchorage, AK: 113 pg.

National Park Service, 1985. "Trip Report Memorandum, Aniakchak NM&P, July 3-13, 1985," prepared by Dave Manski, Natural Resource Specialist Trainee: NPS files, King Salmon, AK.

National Park Service, 1983. "Aniakchak National Monument and Preserve End of Season Report," George Stroud and Lynn Fuller, seasonal rangers: NPS files, King Salmon, AK.

18. Alagnak National Wild River

Mosby, Jack and David Dapkus, 1986. Alaska Paddling Guide, J&R Enterprises, Anchorage, AK: 113 pg.

DOROTHY KEELER

What can I do when they ask me to
describe this land of smokes?
this valley of fire and ice?
How can I explain with words
a thing that is beyond the bounds of word?
My only reply is to close my eyes
and picture those cindered spires
and to simply say: Put your words away,
it must be seen and felt and heard.

Chuck Ash
Baked Mountain Cabin Journal
July 1987